"The extraordinary life o[...] department chaplain, coun[...] [...] LGBTQ people, hero of 9/11— shows us many things. It shows us what it means to live out a religious vocation in the modern world; it shows us how Franciscan spirituality is ever green and ever new; and it shows us, as if we needed any more assurance, that you can be gay and holy."

> —James Martin, SJ, author of *Learning to Pray* and *In All Seasons, For All Reasons*

"A robust and tender volume about a man made infamous in death on 9/11, his body a symbol of that day. From childhood through changes and challenges, DeBernardo skillfully tells the story of Mychal Judge's life. Reminding us that the wounds are where the healing will be, this book is illuminating. DeBernardo reveals the many sides of Judge's true humanity, and his gift of being a most wounded—and skilled—healer."

> —Fran Rossi Szpylczyn, is a freelance writer and retreat leader, and is the pastoral associate for administration at Immaculate Conception in Glenville, New York

"Fr. Mychal Judge became world famous on September 11, 2001, through an iconic photo that symbolized the horror of that day. This book is the story of the generous-hearted, compassionate Franciscan friar behind the photo. It is what we need in a divisive time to renew our own paths to community."

> —Simone Campbell, SSS

"This book provides readers with a window into the life, the mind and, most movingly, the heart of Father Mychal Judge. Many know the Franciscan friar's name because of his heroic last day of Christian ministry to and with the victims of the September 11 attacks, but few know about the many decades of life that preceded it. Francis DeBernardo shares the very human story of a very holy man whose struggles and challenges were as significant in his Christian journey as any success or accomplishment. This book will deepen your appreciation for the life and legacy of Father Mychal Judge."

> —Daniel P. Horan, OFM, Professor and Director of the Center for Spirituality, Saint Mary's College, Notre Dame, Indiana

People of God

Remarkable Lives, Heroes of Faith

People of God is a series of inspiring biographies for the general reader. Each volume offers a compelling and honest narrative of the life of an important twentieth- or twenty-first-century Catholic. Some living and some now deceased, each of these women and men has known challenges and weaknesses familiar to most of us but responded to them in ways that call us to our own forms of heroism. Each offers a credible and concrete witness of faith, hope, and love to people of our own day.

Mychal Judge

Take Me Where You Want Me to Go

Francis DeBernardo

LITURGICAL PRESS
Collegeville, Minnesota

www.litpress.org

Cover design by Red+Company. Cover illustration by Philip Bannister.

© 2022 by Francis DeBernardo
Published by Liturgical Press, Collegeville, Minnesota. All rights reserved.
No part of this book may be used or reproduced in any manner whatsoever,
except brief quotations in reviews, without written permission of Liturgical
Press, Saint John's Abbey, PO Box 7500, Collegeville, MN 56321-7500.
Printed in the United States of America.

1   2   3   4   5   6   7   8   9

Library of Congress Control Number: 2020935175

ISBN 978-0-8146-4420-1   978-0-8146-4444-7 (e-book)

In memory of my parents,
Anna, Celia, Jim,
who also gave their lives completely

Contents

Acknowledgments

I would like to thank the following people for their assistance in completing this project:

Father Joseph Nagle, OFM, and Brother Thomas Barton, OSF, for providing direction on Franciscan formation and spirituality.

James Gormally, a fellow writer, who allowed me to share my struggles with him.

Dr. Jerry Fath, a psychotherapist, for reviewing material on addiction and the AA movement.

Yvonne Altman O'Connor, for her genealogical research in Ireland of Mychal Judge's ancestry.

Shannon Chisholm, Hans Christoffersen, Peter Dwyer, Barry Hudock, and Stephanie Lancour, editors who provided patient guidance, support, and expertise.

My colleagues at New Ways Ministry—Dwayne Fernandes; Sister Jeannine Gramick, SL; Kevin C Molloy; Matthew Myers; Robert Shine—for allowing me the time and space to work on this book.

Michael Ford, for his fraternal encouragement.

Jocelyn Thomas, communications director of the Holy Name Province of the Order of Friars Minor, for connecting me with Franciscan friends who knew Fr. Judge.

And Flannery O'Connor, who advised: "I'm a full-time believer in writing habits, pedestrian as it all may sound. . . . I write only about two hours every day because that's all the energy I have, but I don't let anything interfere with those two hours, at the same time and the same place. This doesn't mean I produce much out of the two hours. Sometimes I work for months and have to throw everything away, but I don't think any of that was time wasted. Something goes on that makes it easier when it does come well. And the fact is if you don't sit there every day, the day it would come well, you won't be sitting there."

CHAPTER ONE

Brooklyn Boy

An Irish Childhood

Although Mychal Judge was born in Brooklyn, New York, he might as well have been born in Ireland. In the midst of a city that defined the modern world, Judge was raised in a world of traditional culture that reflected small-town Irish life. The seeds of his adult life were planted and grew among the sidewalk cracks of New York City, much like the seeds sown in those days by farmers of County Leitrim, from which his parents emigrated, grew in the region's rocky, hardscrabble land. Ireland and New York City were two gravitational pulls that shaped and directed most of Judge's personality, identity, and spirituality.

His Irish roots began with his parents, both of whom came from long-established farming families. Mary Ann Fallon came from the village of Kilmore, and Michael Judge was from Keshcarrigan, in the same county, but about fifty miles apart from each other. In 1921, they met on the steamship that was bringing them both across the Atlantic Ocean to the new world of dreams. Like most European immigrants

1

of the time, they both were looking for a better life than their homeland could offer. Michael's families were farmers, and Mary Ann had served in the Cumann na mBan, the Irish Republican Army women's division, and later worked as a domestic. When they arrived in the United States, great opportunity was not abundant, nor did their steamship introduction immediately blossom. They ended up settling in separate cities: Mary Ann in Brooklyn, working as a domestic, and Michael in Providence, Rhode Island, employed as a laborer. On weekends, Michael would visit Brooklyn and walk up and down past the home where Mary Ann worked, waiting for both the courage and opportunity to speak with her. After an eight-year courtship, they were married on August 30, 1929, at St. Anselm's Parish in the Bay Ridge neighborhood of Brooklyn, a strongly immigrant Irish community.

After marriage, the Judges set up household near downtown Brooklyn, in what is now known as the Cobble Hill neighborhood. It was an enclave for European immigrants, many from Ireland. Their home was not far from the waterfront that overlooked the lower tip of Manhattan where the World Trade Center would eventually be built decades later. The center of the neighborhood community was St. Paul's Church on Congress Street, built a century earlier on land donated by Cornelius Heeney, the wealthy Irish immigrant who also donated the land for Manhattan's St. Patrick's Cathedral, the strongest and most enduring symbol of Irish identity in New York City.

Very quickly, the Judge family began to grow. After a year of marriage, the couple had a daughter, Erin. A few years later, a son, Thomas Emmett, was born, but he died at fifteen months from an ear infection that spread to his mastoid bone. On May 11, 1933, Mary Ann again went into labor, and the future Franciscan was born. Her labor, though, would not end until two days later when his fraternal twin sister, Dympna, was born on May 13.

The history of Ireland's political struggles had a role in the young boy's name. He was baptized Robert Emmett Judge, for the early-nineteenth-century Irish patriot Robert Emmet, who, though Anglican, sympathized with his Catholic countrymen and helped lead a rebellion against the British in 1803. The Judge family called the young boy "Emmett." ("Mychal" would come years later, after a few name changes in religious life.)

Perhaps it was the fabled "luck of the Irish" that helped the family just a year after the twins were born. They had a winning ticket in the Irish Sweepstakes, which had been established just four years earlier by the Irish government to benefit Irish hospitals, with tickets sold around the world. The prize of 514 Irish pounds (around fifty thousand US dollars today) was enough to allow the family to own two luxuries that most immigrants could only dream of: a car and a house.

Like many Catholic immigrants, the family's life was centered around the local parish, which helped them maintain strong ties to old world traditions. While faith was central to their lives and identity, Mary Ann, who became a full-time homemaker after marriage, did not have the fearful respect for the clergy that many Irish immigrants had. She believed the local Irish clergy should have provided more comforting pastoral care to parishioners instead of the strict rules that they enforced. It was not uncommon for her to strongly criticize the pope, bishops, priests, nuns—a forthrightness almost unheard of from devout Catholics of that era but perhaps not surprising from a veteran of the Cumann na mBan.

Criticism of the church's leaders did not interfere with her deep and abiding Catholic faith. Praying was a continuous part of Mary Ann's day, her prayers repeated softly, rhythmically, under her breath. The future priest would later describe how his mother's prayer form "had a rhythm to it, a magic to it," and that "somehow it became part of me."[1] Her connection to God was intimate and personal. Church structures were superfluous to her expression of faith.

Mary Ann's antagonism toward clerical figures could only mean that she must have been filled with great consternation when the toddler Emmett, when asked about his dreams for the future, routinely would answer, "I wanna be a peest."[2] Despite his inability to correctly pronounce the word *priest*, his decisiveness about a clerical vocation was early, strong, and lasting.

Emmett's father presented a different side of the Irish personality than Mary Ann did. Hardly rebellious, Michael had chosen not to fight militarily in the struggles for Ireland's independence from the British. The elder Judge's connection to the land was less political and more poetic: he was full of music and stories, magic and myth. From early on in Emmett's life, his father's melodies and lyrics about Ireland's heroes, legends, and landscapes danced in the young boy's imagination. Emmett's lifelong love of Irish ballads and his naturally florid ability with language no doubt came from the Judge side of the family.

This Irish consciousness also imbued in him the seamless connection between the sacred and secular. Celtic myth saw the world as infused with the divine, and the Christianization of the Irish nation continued to propagate this awareness. Holiness existed naturally, not supernaturally. Prayers and blessings were not something reserved only for church on Sunday, but they were part of the daily routines of school, play, work, family, and neighborhood. Prayer, as his mother's example showed, was as natural as breathing.

When Emmett was three years old, his father was diagnosed with mastoiditis, a serious infection of the middle and inner ear—the same condition that had claimed the life of his first son. Complications to this condition can cause blood clots in the brain, vision and hearing loss, facial paralysis, and meningitis. He was admitted to St. Peter's Hospital, just a few blocks from the family's home, and remained under treatment there for three years. Perhaps worse than the pain and weakness, his three children were not allowed to visit him.

Emmett's only connection with his father during this three-year period was occasionally waving to him from the sidewalk as the frail man stood at the window of his hospital room. Throughout his life, Judge always imagined God as a caring father who looked over him. In effect, this was the way that he remembered much of his childhood with his biological father.

Despite nine surgeries, many treatments, and continuous care for three years, Michael Judge did not recover. He died on June 2, 1939, when Emmett was six years old.

The loss was profound for the young boy. Becoming fatherless affected his spiritual imagination in a unique way. The concept of a loving God can be a challenge for many because God is also imagined as physically distant and intangible. However, Emmett's earthly father was also an absent presence in his life, so it was not a big leap to imagine a similarly loving but untouchable Godhead. In adulthood, Judge reflected on how the loss of his father deepened a personal relationship with God: "I've grown up with this God, and I've always loved Him. For years I feared Him, but I always talked to Him because there was no father, no uncles, no brothers, no cousins. So God was the man in my life, and very often because He was the man—He was older—I was afraid of Him. But I knew that somehow He would take care of me, and He did."[3]

Emmett's childhood years were spent at St. Paul's Parish school, run by the Sisters of Charity, and he served as an altar boy at the church. According to Dympna, he was not one of the brighter students in their class, but he worked hard. She also described his faith as "intuitive." She said, "It wasn't three Our Fathers and three Hail Marys. It had nothing to do with what we learned in school or at home. It came out of him."[4]

Frank Murphy, a friend from childhood with whom Judge stayed in contact throughout his life, recalled how the two boys, both sons of Irish immigrants, grew up in a world guarded by traditions and responsibilities. Murphy recalled: "We had the Irish ethic, peculiar to New York and to the part of Brooklyn we were from, of very strong traditions, belief in respecting authority, a strong relationship with the church, and that dear old Catholic secrecy. 'What'll the neighbors say? Never let anybody know anything bad that's going on.'"[5]

Of course, Irish guilt and doom were also part of this heritage. Judge recalled that when the family drove past the infamous Sing Sing Prison outside New York City, his mother would warn the children that this institution was the destination for those who did not attend Catholic school. His twin, Dympna, remembered being terrified by such warnings, but she recalled that Emmett was more immune to such threats. Guilt instilled in him an immense, sometimes oppressive sense of responsibility. In later life, Judge would say that he always felt he could be doing more for people, that whatever he did was not good enough.

A New York Childhood

While traditional Irish Catholic culture formed the young Judge's personality, habits, and values, he was not raised in a bucolic, whitewashed cottage with a thatched roof surrounded by green fields and peat bogs. The culture of the fast-paced, gritty streets of New York City would also shape his spirituality and outlook on life. New York's traffic sounds, roaring subways, and boisterous crowds would be his childhood's background soundtrack instead of lilting Irish ballads. Emmett grew up amid bustling urban clamor, and he would be energized by that hustle and bustle all his life. In New York City, one was never physically far from some of the nation's most powerful financial and political leaders or from the nation's most destitute citizens. Emmett grew up surrounded by and keenly aware of both populations.

The Judge family lived at 230 Dean Street, a modest row house. While his street was residential in character, he was only a few blocks away from the intersection of Flatbush and Atlantic Avenues, often referred to as the Times Square of Brooklyn. These two major thoroughfares, which in separate routes went from one end of the borough to the other, were lined with stores and office buildings. A few blocks in the opposite direction led to the Brooklyn Piers, an industrial area where ships from around the world deposited cargo containers by the dozen each day. His home was also not far from the governmental center of Borough Hall and Brooklyn's courts.

Just about a mile from where Emmett was raised stood the Brooklyn Bridge, the nineteenth century's greatest engineering feat, an elegant display of stone towers and intricate cable work that continues to inspire artists, writers, and ordinary folk. The bridge connects the humming world of sophisticated Manhattan with the only slightly less humming world of the humbler borough of Brooklyn. Judge walked the pedestrian planks thousands of times, both as a boy and an adult. The Brooklyn Bridge would be for him a sort of a spiritual touchtone, a place of retreat, for his entire life.

Like any true Brooklynite of the era, Emmett was a devotee of the borough's other great "religious" institution: the Brooklyn Dodgers baseball team. It's hard to overestimate the communal spirit that the Brooklyn Dodgers engendered in this borough brimming with humanity and with a passion for underdogs. The immense diversity of the city's ethnic, religious, racial, and social classes disappeared at the entrance gates to Ebbets Field, the team's hallowed stadium. The Dodgers would lead America in the great struggle for racial integration. In 1947, when Emmett was fourteen years old and already a die-hard fan, they hired the first black professional baseball player, Jackie Robinson.

The team was also known, during Judge's later childhood and teen years, for breaking their fans' hearts by so frequently winning their league's pennant but then, with only one exception in 1955, falling in defeat (each time to the New York Yankees) in the subsequent World Series. They were perpetual underdogs. Emmett's favorite player would also become the most vilified Dodger. Pitcher Ralph Branca earned an ignominious place in baseball history as the man who delivered the ball to New York Giants slugger Bobby Thompson that resulted in the famous home run—"the shot heard 'round the world"—that cost the Dodgers the just-within-reach championship in 1951. One of the few worldly possessions that Judge took with him to seminary was a framed photo of Branca.

Though Brooklyn's concrete sidewalks, asphalt streets, and adjoined tenement homes were a far cry from the Emerald Isle, what the two locales had in common was shaky economic conditions. Winning the Irish Sweepstakes had been a one-time windfall for the family, but as the Depression worsened, they would have just been able to make ends meet on Michael Judge's salary as a clerk for a local supermarket chain. His long illness would have only worsened their economic status.

After Michael's death in 1939, Mary Ann began to take in boarders to help pay the bills. As with so many families during the Depression, the Judge children were expected to contribute to the family income. Emmett and a friend took up shoe shining, peddling their services near New York's Pennsylvania Railroad Station. This great faucet that poured people into Manhattan was one of the busiest spots in the city, but there was an oasis of peace nearby that would play a determinative role in this Catholic boy's life.

St. Francis of Assisi Church on West 31st Street, just a short walk from the station, became a regular destination for young Emmett. Since he was already familiar with riding the subway to the Pennsylvania Station neighborhood, the Sisters of Charity enlisted him as an errand boy. Whenever a death occurred, they sent him to this Franciscan parish to purchase a Mass card.

By the time of the Depression, St. Francis of Assisi Church already had a long and well-deserved reputation for being a place where anyone, rich or poor, could go for a moment of prayer amid the noise and car exhaust of the interminable pulse of midtown Manhattan. Frequent daily Masses and the sacrament of reconciliation, then known as "confession," were the main ministries conducted by the Franciscan Friars of the Holy Name Province who served the parish.

The church building was wedged between Herald Square, where Macy's and Gimbels attracted the city's highest commercial traffic, and Pennsylvania Station, the city's main gateway. It was also the home of St. Anthony's Breadline, established in 1929 after the stock market crash. Homeless people knew they could get a free daily meal there. Poverty and despair were adjacent to capitalism and power. St. Francis was a place to be refreshed in the midst of the height of urban confusion and depersonalization.

The Franciscan church was much more spectacular than his familiar neighborhood parish church of St. Paul's. The backdrop of the sanctuary was a mosaic of Mary, Queen of the Order of Friars Minor, which included a long line of Franciscan saints in its tiles. At the time, it was the largest mosaic in the United States. Throughout both the upper and lower churches were other radiant mosaics depicting the Assumption of the Blessed Virgin Mary, the Death of St. Joseph, St. Anthony, the Sorrowful Mother, and St. Francis in Glory.

While these images must have awed the young boy, something else attracted him to this church. Fr. Henry Vincent Lawler, OFM, greeted the boy one day and spoke with him kindly and gently. Emmett was enthralled by the priest, and he began to follow him on church errands and tasks whenever he visited. Years later, Judge fondly recalled this friendly, happy priest: "There was something simple and beautiful about him. Watching him, I realized that I didn't care for material things all that much. I would just walk around and follow him and I loved his brown robe and sandals. I knew then that I wanted to be a friar."[6]

Emmett was hooked. As a teenager he entered St. Francis Preparatory School in Brooklyn, run not by the Order of Friars Minor but by the Franciscan Brothers of Brooklyn, a Third Order community established by Franciscans from Ireland. The academic rigor and discipline was tough, especially since he was not an outstanding student, but Emmett did not endure the crucible for long. During his freshman year, against the wishes of his mother, Emmett applied for membership in the Holy Name Province of the Order of Friars Minor. His mother tried to dissuade him, but he was fixed. "Let him go and let him find out," she eventually decided.

In the early fall of 1948, at the age of fifteen, Emmett Judge left Brooklyn by subway and railroad for St. Joseph Seraphic Seminary in Callicoon, New York, about 120 miles northwest. He left home carrying just one suitcase. The date was September 11.

Franciscan Adulthood

Callicoon, New York, is a peaceful hamlet situated at a bend in the Delaware River, which serves as the border between Pennsylvania and the Empire State. In 1948, when Emmett Judge arrived there, its heyday as a small hub for the modest farming and lumber communities in the region had long since passed. Looming high over the lazy river bend was the imposing St. Joseph's Seraphic Seminary, a Franciscan boarding school, which would be Judge's home over the next six years. It was in these walls made of native bluestone that the teenage Judge would mature as a person, as a Catholic, and as a candidate for the Province of the Holy Name.

Although the institution was called a seminary, technically, it was a minor seminary: a school whose curriculum encompassed high school and the first two years of college. Beyond the academics, the students were also beginning the process of formation as Franciscans, learning about Catholicism and the history, traditions, and spirituality of the religious order founded by St. Francis, the poor man from Assisi whose mission was nothing less than rebuilding the church. For the next thirteen years, as Judge progressed from minor seminary to novitiate to first vows and scholasticate to major seminary to solemn vows and finally to ordination, he would be formed in a spirituality, which, in addition to his Irish culture and New York sensibility, would set a trajectory for his future ministries.

Religious formation in the pre-Vatican II church of the 1950s was a highly rigid and rigorous process. It was governed by rules, rubrics, and routines. Very little deviated from the daily and annual schedules. And very little of a person's behavior was not governed by some dictate that was to be observed meticulously. For Judge, the rigor may have seemed like a case of "out of the frying pan, into the fire," since he had not been happy at the strictly regulated Catholic high school he attended for one year before his move to Callicoon. At least there he could return home to his mother and sisters at the end of each afternoon and enjoy a bit of freedom. At St. Joseph's, even at fifteen, his life was governed by a regimen from which there was little place for spontaneous, youthful exuberances.

The schedule was demanding. Morning rising was at 4:45 a.m., and after splashing some water on their faces, the boys went to chapel, where they participated in the Liturgy of the Hours (then called the Divine Office), meditation, and Mass, until about 7:30 a.m. All of the rituals were conducted in Latin, which the boys were still learning in their daily classes. After a brief time for daily hygiene, breakfast followed, and like most meals, it was held in silence. Afterward, the school day followed, with a standard curriculum, though one executed with an overlay of religious piety wherever possible.

When classes ended, the boys were allowed time for recreation, which consisted mostly of sports and athletic activities. Judge was not skilled in these areas, and he didn't have a passion for competition as some of the other young teens did. Emmett was more musically inclined, as well as a natural entertainer. So, despite his lack of athletic enthusiasm, he would not have been alone or ostracized. He had an outgoing personality that helped him to naturally develop amicable relationships with a wide circle of his confreres. And even at this early age, he was a master of humor, song, and entertainment—gifts inherited from his Irish upbringing that would serve him well in building relationships as an adult and as a pastoral minister. He got along well with his schoolmates and enjoyed the camaraderie of community life, which he would treasure throughout his life.

The evening began with chapel prayer, followed by dinner, again in silence, social recreation, study hall, night prayer, and then off to sleep in a huge dormitory where each student had little more than a bed and a small cabinet for clothes, books, and few personal effects.

While they were not isolated from their families, contact was strictly regulated. Visits home occurred at Thanksgiving, Christmas, Easter, and for the whole summer. One of his jobs during the summer, to pay for his schooling, was to dig graves in New York's St. John's Cemetery where his father was buried.

Whenever they left the school to travel, they wore a white shirt and all black clothing: jacket, pants, necktie, socks, shoes. Perhaps the somber clothing was intended to make them less noticeable to girls, whom they were constantly admonished to avoid. Similarly, they were warned against forming "particular friendships" with their classmates, for fear of stimulating homosexual relationships. No evidence exists that Judge violated relationship boundaries set by either of these warnings.

How did young Judge respond to the expectation of celibacy during formation, as he prepared to eventually take a vow to live as such? Not much is known, though later in life, when Judge kept a personal journal, he reflected at one point on his adolescence. He recalled the confusion about his emerging gay sexual feelings. He was not sure what they meant, but he was certain that he was the only one feeling them. Given what he saw as his human failing of not always choosing well, he marveled at his ability to remain celibate year after year.[7]

While Judge liked the camaraderie of communal living, like all human beings he had his periods of loneliness. The formation program's emphasis on selflessness and of not being a problem for others was easily interpreted as a requirement not to express personal problems and issues—especially for someone who had been taught from a young age to keep any problems and potential embarrassments or weaknesses to himself. One way that Judge dealt with his loneliness and inability to express emotions during this period was with alcohol.

Judge's dependence on alcohol began with sneaking sips of altar wine.[8] Like many budding alcoholics, he became skilled at hiding his cravings and use, not appearing as a slurring, sloppy drunkard, but maintaining a façade of serenity.[9]

In 1954, when Judge was twenty-one years old, he graduated from the minor seminary and entered the novitiate at St. Bonaventure Monastery in Paterson, New Jersey. This passage marked his official entry into the Franciscan community. On being received into the order, novices took on a religious name, signaling a new identity. Robert Emmett Judge combined his mother's maiden name and his father's given name to become known as Fallon Michael. *Fallon* was put first because there were already many brothers named Michael in the community. Yet soon after he received the new name, he wrote to his provincial asking to reverse the order, since he had been his father's only son and wanted to honor his name. He was allowed to do so.

After taking first vows in August 1955, Judge was sent to St. Francis College in Rye, New York, where he completed his undergraduate studies in philosophy. Two years later, he began his four-year course in theology at Holy Name College, Washington, DC. In both of these settings, as in high school, academics were not Judge's forte. His understanding and love of his faith was more personal, practical, and intuitive than it was intellectual.

Michael Fallon Judge was ordained a priest on February 25, 1961, at the Franciscan Monastery of the Holy Land in America, a shrine next door to Holy Name College. Archbishop Egidio Vagnozzi, the Vatican's apostolic delegate to the United States, ordained him along with the rest of his confreres. The next day, he celebrated his first Mass at his home parish, St. Paul's, in Brooklyn. Thus his journey came full circle. Formed by Ireland, Brooklyn, and Franciscan spirituality, he was ready to begin his priestly ministry.

The religious formation process had been like a double-edged sword for Judge. It provided him with spiritual tools and insights that would serve him well in his ministry throughout his life. Yet the patterns of the process also allowed him, perhaps even encouraged him, to repress certain parts of his personality, causing severe existential pain. His friend Steven Weaver captured this duplicity of effect when he recalled that Judge experienced formation "like a hairshirt that he had to wear close to his skin. It would always prevent him from being 'truly real and present.' At the same time, it helped him appreciate the image of Francis embracing the figure of Christ on the cross, and he strove to reproduce it in his own life."[10]

As the cross was not the end for Christ, it was not the end for Michael Judge either. But as he proceeded from formation into pastoral ministry, he would first enter deeper into personal suffering, masked by a façade of buoyant workaholism that was too often encouraged and rewarded in church life. But resurrection and new life waited beyond those torments too.

CHAPTER TWO

Parish Priest

Ordinary Time

The priestly ministry of the man who died heroically aiding those in a catastrophe that rocked the globe started as ordinarily as it does for most priests: he was assigned to parish work. After ordination in 1961, and for more than the next two decades, Fr. Michael Fallon Judge's primary pastoral tasks were to maintain the regular rounds of Mass celebrations, confessions, home and hospital visits, baptisms, weddings, funerals, and one-on-one counseling sessions that almost every priest experiences.

The Franciscan Holy Name Province ministered in dioceses throughout New England, the Northeast, and mid-Atlantic regions, staffing parishes in cities and suburbs. His first assignment was an internship year of urban ministry at St. Anthony's Shrine in downtown Boston, a church that primarily serves people working in the city's center, as well as those living in the alleys and streets of the downtown area. It would have been a very familiar setting, because its demographics and ministries were similar to St. Francis of

Assisi parish, the midtown Manhattan church where he first encountered the Franciscans as a young boy. The mission provided him ample opportunity to learn the basics of priestly ministry.

At the end of the year, Michael was reassigned to St. Joseph's Parish in East Rutherford, New Jersey, and most of his life's priestly ministry would take place in the Garden State. For most of the next two decades, Michael worked in largely middle-class, suburban communities. His other parish assignments were at Sacred Heart in nearby Rochelle Park and St. Joseph's in West Milford.

The young priest immediately took to parish life. Naturally outgoing, handsome, and friendly, with a gift for making people feel comfortable around him, Michael had no problem developing relationships with parishioners. His broad smile and easy laugh quickly made him a favorite of all, young and old. Although most Catholics of the era held priests on pedestals, Michael intentionally worked against that glorified image, letting people know that he was as down-to-earth and human as they were.

By all accounts, Fr. Michael's genius was in making friends. He could strike up a conversation with anyone and everyone, and he left all feeling better about themselves. John and Arlene Barone were young newlywed parishioners in East Rutherford when Judge arrived there. They were astonished at this new type of priest who spoke to people conversationally and who was disposed to point out the good, rather than the bad, in each person. "He knew everybody's name and would not forget them," John said. "He wanted to know all about you, your family, and what was important for you. It was like he was a member of the family, and everyone thought he was a member of their families, too."[1]

Judge's casual style and affirming manner made him immediately appealing to the youth of the parishes where he served. He sported a 1960s-style shaggy hairdo that may have shocked some parishioners used to more clean-cut priests, but which may have helped him relate a bit more comfortably with young people. His preference for wearing jeans and t-shirts when not in habit also added to this image. "He was like a movie star!" recalled Eugene Dermody, Jr., who was a young teen when Judge was ministering in East Rutherford.[2] Dermody recalled that Judge soon became the coordinator of youth activities at the parish. He opened the parish's lyceum, a large auditorium/gymnasium for socials and activities, on weekend nights, giving the young a place to gather.

Judge's ministry was not all fun and games, though. Growing up, Dermody had difficulties with autism and dyslexia (both undiagnosed at the time), causing many behavioral problems in school and frustrating his parents and teachers alike. Having run out of options, his parents would send him to talk with Judge. Unlike the other adults, the priest patiently listened to the youth's frustrations with school and peers. Instead of being judgmental or stern with the teen, Judge simply told him, "I see good things in you." Thanks in part to the priest's encouragement, Dermody went from a failing student to the honor roll.[3]

Judge's patience helped Dermody with another important aspect of his life that none of the adults around him understood at the time. As a young teenager, Dermody began to develop crushes on boys that he knew. He soon began to be teased and bullied by his peers. The adults around him didn't know how to respond. Judge stepped in and provided the teenager with support and information he needed. The priest explained the "facts of life" to Dermody in a very honest, nonchalant tone. Concerning Dermody's responses to other boys, Judge told the youth, "This is nothing to beat yourself up about." He reassured him that his feelings were natural and nothing to fear. "I know more about you than you know about yourself," the priest reassured him. "He seemed to know I was gay even before I did," Dermody remembers.[4]

Joseph Tereskiewicz, a parishioner at St Joseph's Parish in West Milford, New Jersey, said that Judge made an indelible impression on him when the priest showed up at Tereskiewicz's father's wake. Joe and his wife, Susan, were new to the parish and did not know any of the pastoral staff well. They had not requested a priest for the wake because the funeral home was forty-five minutes away. Judge, however, had seen the obituary in the newspaper and recognized the parishioner's name, so he took it upon himself to make the trip to pay a visit. "Who's this?" Tereskiewicz remembers thinking when the robed friar entered the room, not familiar enough with the priest to recognize him from the parish.

"He came over and offered his condolences," Tereskiewicz said. "Then he went over to the casket and prayed for my father. He then touched my father's hands and said, 'These were the hands of a hard-working man, a carpenter.' I was amazed that he knew this." Tereskiewicz, himself a heavy equipment mechanic, was impressed at Judge's concern for working people.[5]

Father Mike soon became known for his unique style of preaching. Even before liturgical rubrics relaxed after the Second Vatican Council, he would move away from the pulpit, descend the steps of the sanctuary, and preach amid the congregation, sometimes walking up and down the aisle. His content was filled with examples from ordinary life. His wry Irish sense of humor peppered these homilies, making people laugh and feel comfortable in church. "It was like he was having a conversation with his friends," Tereskiewicz explained.[6] The congregations were rapt.

John Barone said that parishioners looked forward to Michael's sermons. "He sounded like an ordinary person, not a priest. Unlike with some other preachers, you didn't want his homilies to end," Barone recalled. "People hung on his every word. He knew everything that was going on in the neighborhood and his homilies often included these topics."[7]

What made his preaching style even more remarkable is that he hardly ever prepared what he was going to say. "What's today's gospel?" he would ask the other friars as he got ready to go over to the church for Mass. Extemporaneous speaking came as naturally to him as did his gift for conversation. In a newspaper interview, Michael described his homiletic approach: "We have to be versatile in preaching. If I'm giving a homily and a fire truck goes by with the ringing siren, I switch my original thoughts and relate to what's happening—the fire—and what could be a distraction becomes an asset."[8]

One older friar wrote to Michael during his early parish ministry and praised the young priest's preaching: "You have the enviable gift of being able to stand up publicly and talk very honestly, sincerely, and naturally, letting the people know that you like them, and that you like God and that you want them to like Him too. You bowled me over Michael."[9]

While Michael could speak well, he was an even better listener. He developed a reputation for being a patient, quiet presence as people struggled to talk about their challenges, doubts, anxieties, and relationships. People knew, too, that they could rely on him making himself available for them. In 1974, a local newspaper article about Judge carried the headline, "The Listening Priest," and the subhead, "A priest who can't say no."[10] Preaching at Judge's funeral Mass, Fr. Michael Duffy, OFM, who had ministered alongside Michael, remembered his gift for listening and simply being present:

> While the rest of us were running around organizing altar boys and choirs and liturgies and decorations, he was in his office listening. His heart was open. His ears were open and especially he listened to people with problems.

He carried around with him an appointment book. He had appointments to see people four and five weeks in advance. He would come to the rec room at night at 11:30, having just finished his last appointment, because when he related to a person, they felt like he was their best friend.[11]

This constant availability, however, eventually took a toll on Michael. Seventeen-hour days were not unusual, and one account from 1976 says fourteen-hour days were the norm.[12] In 1966, while at St. Joseph's in East Rutherford, he suffered a breakdown that manifested itself in physical paralysis that doctors determined was psychological in origin. In addition to the exhaustion, his community life at this time had not been satisfying. He seemed to be incompatible with the other friars in his community. Perhaps some resented his popularity among the parishioners. Perhaps Michael's outsized personality made him difficult to live with. Franciscan Father Richard Rohr speculated that "his style and freedom may have been a point of envy for other people."[13] Whatever the reason for his exhaustion and unsatisfying relationships, Michael had given more to others than he gave to himself, an occupational hazard for pastoral ministers.

After a hospital stay and several months of sabbatical, Michael returned to parish ministry in 1967 at Sacred Heart in Rochelle Park. The pastor there was Father Henry Lawler, OFM, the same priest whom young Emmett had met in Manhattan on his visits to St. Francis of Assisi Church.

Franciscan Spirit

Michael's pastoral ministry style sprung not only from his personality and social talent but from the Franciscan spirituality that shaped his understanding of God. Primary among these Franciscan spiritual values is a deep reverence for the incarnation of Christ. St. Francis was so taken with the idea that God took on human flesh, became human, and entered history that he wanted people to have a strong visual reminder of the event. He is credited with having started the now universal tradition of erecting a nativity scene at Christmas time.

But in Franciscan thought, the incarnation was more than just something that happened once in Bethlehem over two thousand years ago. For the poor man from Assisi and his followers through the centuries, *all* of creation was a reflection of God's glory. Nothing earthly is foreign to God. All is essentially good. The incarnation is a way of looking at and receiving the world and its people.

Though many have tamed this Franciscan value into sentimental thoughts about the beauty of nature, the emphasis on the immanence of God in the world became a grounding principle for how the friars ministered.

His friend Brian Carroll, who had been a friar, recalled that Michael "fell in love with St. Francis."[14] As a priest, Michael took it upon himself to point out the fusion of the divine and the human in each individual life. God was not distant but was down in the dirt. God was not something to be achieved, but was already active in people's lives, actions, and relationships. For Michael, being a pastoral minister meant seeing God acting in every person's life. He had a keen sense of the connection between the secular and the sacred, the divine and the human, the mundane and the supernatural. With St. Francis as his model, Michael saw God and goodness everywhere and in everyone, no matter how small or outcast.

He told a local newspaper reporter in 1978, "God is here, right here, alive and with us. God is so tremendously great to me. If he weren't, I couldn't do the things I do. And every time I do something for him, he does so much more for me. Every person has the responsibility to talk about God. When we speak of God, we bring a sense of God, even for a moment, into the world. At the same time, we develop a sense of God in our own lives. God is not an obligation, a burden. God is the joy of my life."[15]

One way his incarnational spirit manifested itself was through Michael's practice of blessing . . . nearly everything. Because everything to him was sacred and should be recognized as such, his blessings were ubiquitous. He blessed pregnant women, sick people, marriages, animals, mealtimes, recreational times. Blessings were not simply spiritual gestures but physical ones, in which he laid hands on a person, hugged them, looked deep in their eyes, made personal contact. His blessings didn't so much evoke a supernatural force as much as recognize and affirm the presence of the divine already working in a person's body, relationships, and event.

Another powerful influence on Michael's pastoral ministry was the Second Vatican Council, which opened the year after he was ordained. The council emphasized the church as actively involved in the world and the lives of its people rather than being a cloistered institution concerned with otherworldly realities. The council humanized the church. Of course, these teachings were not welcomed by all Catholics, but Michael's sister Dympna recalled his reaction to this major renewal of the church: "He *loved* Vatican II."[16] Michael loved the freeing spirit the council provided to pastoral ministers. He said in 1974, "Before Vatican II we were always trying to manage people's lives. Do this. Don't do that. Go to Mass. Don't eat meat on Friday. I was brought up in the old school, and I have to remind myself, 'Mike, let people be.'"[17]

Parishioner Michael Barbire recalled an example of how Judge favored the human and practical over the doctrinaire.

Barbire was attending a civic organization's dinner that ended up posing a problem for the Catholics in attendance since it was a day to abstain from meat, yet prime sirloin was being served. Since Judge was in attendance, they turned to him for guidance. From the podium, he told the assembled diners, "Remember what your mother told you. Eat what's on your plate."[18]

Striving to adopt a more collaborative parish ministry that reflected the council's teaching, Judge convinced his Franciscan leaders to experiment with a new style of parish administration that was becoming popular in the US church in the early 1970s: team ministry. This model allowed priests to share leadership and authority for the parish equally, rather than relying on a hierarchical model with one pastor making all decisions and supervising the parish's other priests. In 1972, St. Joseph's in East Rutherford became the first parish of the Archdiocese of Newark to institute team ministry. "It has nothing to do with rebellion against established authority," he explained to a newspaper reporter. "It's a sharing of responsibilities. Instead of emphasizing our place in the hierarchy, we're emphasizing the quality of our life together, how well we can relate."[19]

Team ministry also emphasized individuality, difference, and communication. "We agree to disagree," Judge explained. "We're six completely different personalities. But each of us can serve the parish in our own way." The new model gave the priests more freedom to take personal responsibility for their ministries—a far cry from the old model where they would need to ask the pastor for permission to make house calls or use a friary car.

Although Michael was energized by the teaching of the council, his enthusiasm for the new did not mean he rejected all of the old ways in which he was spiritually formed. In fact, he continued to observe many of the traditional practices he had learned from the immigrant Catholicism of his childhood. The rosary remained an important part of his prayer ritual for the rest of his life, even though some of his confreres had abandoned it as old-fashioned. Throughout his life, Michael's personal evening prayers were done on his knees at his bedside. He was not a radical who rejected all of the old ways just for the sake of change. He kept what he found spiritually nourishing. With a foot in both ecclesial styles, he was able to help people adjust to the sometimes unsettling and bumpy changes prompted by the council.

Extraordinary Ministry

Fr. Michael's ministry extended beyond the parish boundaries, involving him in a number of civic and diocesan activities. Because of his connection to young people, he was appointed to Bergen County's Juvenile Conference Committee, a service of the juvenile court to help young first-time offenders with minor infractions. In addition, he served as a county coordinator for the Catholic Youth Organization.

Michael also started serving as chaplain to the fire departments of East Rutherford and Carlstadt, New Jersey. His friends say that Michael had always been alert to sirens and would often drop what he was doing to rush off to emergency scenes to see if he could be of help. The opportunity to be of service overruled any sense of danger that these situations held.

In 1974, Michael's involvement in a dangerous situation saved lives and turned him into a local hero. On May 19, Michael learned of a domestic hostage situation in progress in nearby Carlstadt. He rushed to the scene, where he learned that a man named James Hayms had barricaded himself in his house and was holding his wife and two young children at gunpoint, threatening to kill them. Hayms had already shot off several rounds at the crowd of policemen who were at the scene.

Along with a detective and a local judge, Michael began to speak with Hayms on the phone, trying to convince him to surrender. When these pleas proved ineffective, Michael, in Franciscan habit and sandals, climbed a fire ladder to the second story of the home to talk with the man directly through a window.

"You're a good man, James," he said. "You don't need to do this."[20] Hayms allowed Michael to enter the house after the priest offered him a promise that was emblematic of his ministry: "I'll stick by you."

Soon afterward, Michael emerged from the house with the children and then later with the rifle and ammunition. Fr. Michael Duffy, OFM, who was serving in the parish with Judge at the time, recalled that Michael showed no fear during this dangerous ordeal. Michael's promise to the man held true. He remained friends with Hayms throughout the man's prison stay and after his release. In one letter to Michael, Hayms wrote, "You alone have put some meaning in to my life, just the fact that you care . . ."[21]

After this event Judge's renown began to spread through surrounding communities. In a 1974 local newspaper feature about him, Judge reflected on some of his ideas about priestly ministry and the role of the church in the world:

> The hardest lesson I've had to learn in 13 years as a priest is to let people be themselves . . .
> The parish priest is as important as he wants to be. Vatican II put us on the line. In the old days people isolated us on a pedestal. Today, there's a continual challenge for us to do many things, to really be ministers, to bring the sacraments, the Christ life to our people; to counsel—not

to give answers but to counsel. You know there are so many people who have no one to talk to, at least no one to confide in. Sometimes we're merely a sounding board.[22]

The 1960s and 1970s were a time of incredible social and ecclesial upheaval. The Vietnam War, the civil rights movement, and the Second Vatican Council all challenged accepted pieties, secular and sacred. While Michael served at St. Joseph's in East Rutherford, many of the parish's young men were being drafted for military service in southeast Asia, and Michael asked permission of his Franciscan provincial superior to become a military chaplain—a step that could easily have led him to dangerous ministry to American troops in Vietnam. His request was denied, with the provincial saying he was needed at the parish. Michael accepted this decision.[23]

The civil rights movement briefly, but significantly, touched Michael's life at Sacred Heart parish, his second assignment. Michael had been ministering there for only a little over a year when a black family moved into a then all-white neighborhood within the parish. Some of Rochelle Park's citizens, including Sacred Heart parishioners, objected to the family's presence. At the same time, another group of citizens circulated a petition to support and welcome them. Michael signed it. Not everyone was happy with his decision to do so.[24]

Soon after the signature, Michael was suddenly removed from the parish, prompting many to think that his signature on the petition led to his dismissal. Michael spent the next year at St. Francis of Assisi Parish in Manhattan, ministering to the lay Third Order Franciscans who met there. He was then reassigned to St. Joseph's Parish in East Rutherford, much to the delight of both himself and the parishioners.

Workaholic to Alcoholic

The decade of the 1960s was also a time of personal turbulence for many priests and vowed religious men and women. Many opted to leave the ministry, often in order to marry. Two Franciscans who lived in community with Michael and served with him at St. Joseph's were among those who did.

Michael remained committed to priesthood and celibacy. He was not under any misconceptions about the challenge that this life choice presented, especially as middle age inched closer and closer. At one point, he wrote, "For a man to give up the love of a woman, love of children, and love of his home in order to serve the Church, to 'be all things to all men,' as St. Paul says, is a great challenge."[25] Michael saw celibacy as an option that freed him for ministry: "I am freer from family ties. I have more time to serve. My sin is that I don't have enough time."[26]

It appears that during this time he began to acknowledge homosexual feelings to himself and a few others, though it seems he did not see these feelings as primary in his attractions at this point. Father Ron Pecci, OFM, a fellow pastoral minister, recalled that after Michael underwent psychological analysis, he shared that he was neither gay nor straight nor even bisexual. The most accurate description for himself, Michael said, was "omnisexual"—being attracted to all humans.[27]

He was aware, though, of his need for companionship in order to maintain a healthy celibate lifestyle. Referring to interpersonal intimacy, he wrote, "A network of celibate friends . . . is essential for this. I have found the contact must be constant. . . . As long as I share my feelings, I am safe and whole."[28]

During the team ministry experience at the East Rutherford parish, Michael found great camaraderie with the friars. His drinking, however, continued throughout this period. One friar recalled that at night in the friary living room, Michael was always present, laughing with his confreres, sipping from a diet soda can. Fr. Christopher Keenan, OFM, recalled an important detail: "Of course his Tab can was full of scotch."[29]

Judge displayed no signs of drunkenness. Perhaps he did not seek help sooner for his alcoholism because there were no particular incidents or patterns that hampered his life. He didn't crash a car. He didn't oversleep. He never missed Mass or other obligations. Slurred speech and obnoxious behavior were not problems. His alcoholism did not manifest in his social or public life, making it easy to deny that there was a problem at all.

It is difficult to imagine Michael's mind as he ministered generously during the day and evening, while at night, he continually consumed alcohol. It is a pattern that is common for those in ministry who are alcoholic. Alcohol may have helped him relax after a grueling, intense schedule, reducing the inevitable stress of bearing so many people's burdens. It may have helped to deaden the pain of loneliness that can be a common ailment of a celibate life. Perhaps the alcohol helped numb the sadness that may have lingered from the early loss of his father. If he were experiencing inner turmoil about his sexuality, alcohol may have helped to silence those demons. It could have been that he was simply biologically disposed to alcohol addiction and that his youthful stolen sips of altar wine in the sacristy set him on a path that would be difficult to leave. Perhaps it was some mixture of many or all of these or something else entirely. Because he left no explanations of what prompted his addiction to alcohol, it is impossible to know for sure what fueled it.

In 1976, while Michael was still in East Rutherford and before going to the West Milford parish in 1979, he took another break from parish life. A friend of his, Fr. Hugh Hines, OFM, saw that the priest's intense ministry schedule was wearing him down physically and psychologically, and he feared that Michael may have been on his way to another breakdown. So Hines, who was president of Franciscan-run Siena College in Albany, New York, offered Michael a position as his assistant. He accepted.

Michael had recognized the signs of overwork in himself. In a newspaper article about his departure from the parish, he reflected upon his decision: "I believe the Lord is saying, 'All right Michael, here's a chance to become fresh and alive.' All my years in the priesthood have had so much growth, so much fullness, through the good and bad days. My whole life has been with people. In order to continue with people, I need a change. I know this is right what I'm doing." He identified himself at the time with a label that he would believe his whole life long: "I'm a parish priest at heart."[30]

Michael described his new campus responsibilities, in his usual wisecracking way, as doing "whatever the president can't do, won't do, or doesn't want to do."[31] While his duties involved administrative and fundraising work, Michael made each of these tasks into people-oriented jobs. Hines would often delegate to him the task of chairing faculty meetings because Michael was so adept at interacting with people.

Michael naturally turned the position into a pastoral job too. He took on additional duties as the basketball team's chaplain and resided in a women's dormitory to be an on-site mentor and counselor. He continued his natural ministry of being a listening presence, accompanying students, faculty, administrators, and local leaders through whatever challenges they faced.

"He was always late," Hines recalled with a chuckle. "Probably because he always got so involved with people when he was talking with them that he didn't realize the time."[32] Hines began the practice of telling Judge that meetings were beginning earlier than they actually were just to make sure that he would get there on time. When Hines sent Judge to represent the college at a one-on-one luncheon with a state legislator, the meeting was to last no longer than an hour. Judge did not return until after 4:00 p.m., because he and the legislator could not stop chatting.

At Siena, Michael's drinking problem continued unabated. One of his common practices on a night off was to go out for a movie and then head to a bar. The alcoholic patterns started to become obvious to a few friars who knew him well. "I think you're drinking too much," Hines told Judge at one point, hoping to curtail the habit.[33]

Michael also began to see the danger of his drinking pattern, and he decided to challenge himself. In 1978, he went to his first Alcoholics Anonymous meeting, at first just to test the waters, he said. When Michael arrived, he found a fellow Franciscan there. After the meeting, they had a long talk, during which Michael said the four words that would begin his road to recovery: "I am an alcoholic."[34]

CHAPTER THREE

Happy, Joyous, and Free

A New Spirituality

Just as entering Franciscan life directed the future path of young Emmett Judge, so too did Alcoholics Anonymous steer Michael Judge into a new understanding of himself and a new style of ministry. His initial period of recovery serves as a bridge between the two halves of his ministerial life: traditional parish work and outreach to marginalized and specialized groups. This spanning is not a coincidence; the transformation that Judge experienced in recovery inspired and prepared him to move out of traditional expectations into new and cutting-edge areas.

While we have few details about what his actual recovery process entailed, we can safely assume that it involved scores of meetings in church basements or other civic meeting spaces, as well as countless conversations with people at all stages of the recovery process. For the naturally gregarious Judge, who thrived on connections with others, such a fellowship was a perfect fit. We know from reports of friends and from his own self-reporting that for the rest of his life he remained a faithful attendee at AA meetings wherever he was in the world. The meetings became as frequent and regular a habit as prayer had always been for him.

Judge, who thrived in the egalitarian team ministry model in parish work, took well to the anarchic structure of AA. No leaders or authorities exist in the fellowship. Every person directs their own recovery with the aid of a sponsor, a person who is also in recovery, though with more experience. No doubt the simplicity of the AA approach appealed to this priest who had not been a top student and who preferred practical remedies to theological discussions. As he described the program to a young alcoholic: "All you have to do is not drink tonight, wake up tomorrow, go to a meeting, and give me a call."[1] Similar words had been spoken to him when he attended his first AA meeting in 1978 in Albany, New York.

But even though a person in AA will learn simple tips about how to avoid bars and other places where alcohol is poured freely, the 12 Steps that are the heart of the program involve the alcoholic in a deep personal and spiritual transformation. While AA meetings are often hosted by churches and religious organizations, the fellowship is not officially connected in any way to a particular faith. The 12 Steps are not based on any particular theology or religious doctrine. They are offered as guides and tools to help the alcoholic "recover" a true self that has been obscured by excessive habitual use of alcohol. In addition to recovering a more authentic identity, the AA member will also learn and practice new ways of being more honest with self and with other people. Both of these possibilities are facilitated by developing a humble relationship with God or a Higher Power.

The 12-Step process also helps alcoholics examine aspects of their lives that they have long tried to avoid or repress. The AA fellowship provides a supportive environment of peers to help alcoholics discover and heal the inner wounds or predispositions that had encouraged them to seek alcohol for solace or escape in the first place. Because each person's individual story involves different hurts, pains, and struggles, each person's recovery process is a unique and intimate journey.

Judge's recovery involved reconciling with his own brokenness, something he would have first come to terms with in Step 1, in which the alcoholic acknowledges powerlessness. By this point in his life, Judge had already experienced some profound personal challenges: the early death of his father, the overwork of ministry, an emotional breakdown, loneliness while longing for connection, and perhaps other internal conflicts known only to him. His friend Brian Carroll later said that AA helped heal the shame Judge had earlier felt about his sexuality. "The AA experience was part and parcel of his coming out," Carroll recalled. "He was able to accept his authentic self, to see the broken parts of his life as blessings."[2] Recovery helped to make him whole, Carroll said, accepting himself the way God had created him. Given the intense self-examination that AA required, it would have been difficult for Judge *not* to have addressed his sexuality, such an important part of any person's life.

Many gay and lesbian people who have been deeply closeted for a long time report that it was not until involvement with a 12-Step program that they first began to fully acknowledge, accept, and affirm their sexual identities. For many gay and lesbian people of Judge's era, denying or repressing sexuality was a common form of self-protection against social ostracism and even violence. With little information about homosexuality available at the time (and even less for someone in religious life), even simply understanding sexual feelings that were not supported in the wider culture would have been extremely confusing.

For Catholics, the stigma of a gay orientation was greatly increased by the many negative messages about homosexuality they received from their church. The reigning presumption of many in the general public and particularly in the church was that people were heterosexually oriented but that some people freely chose to act homosexually, against their "natural" condition. Homosexuality was not considered a part of one's personal constitution, so it was often assumed that homosexual desires could be controlled by one's will. Not controlling them was a moral failure. The fear, guilt, and shame they would have felt internally, even if they never acted on their desires, only increased the psychic pressure upon them. Unfortunately, a common response pattern was to turn to addictive or other self-destructive behaviors as a way of coping with these social and psychic harms.

Priests or those connected institutionally to the church suffered additional confusion and conflicts about their identities. In vowed religious communities, homosexuality was even more taboo than it was in secular society, so Judge did not have the opportunities to reflect much about his sexuality. Instead of understanding or fully realizing what their sexual identity was, members of religious communities were provided with a sexual identity: celibate. In the formation program that Judge experienced, along with that identity came the usually unspoken message that part of being a celibate was not acknowledging any sexual feelings and believing that sexuality was not an important part of one's personal development. Sexual feelings and sexuality were for laypeople, or, even more specifically, married laypeople.

As a result, many young men who experienced that formation system were very likely unaware of their sexual identity until they became older. The lack of available information about homosexuality at that time, along with the strong social stigma attached to it, would have made it difficult for someone to truly understand what a gay orientation was. Many looked on any same-sex attractions and desires as sinful or, at best, a passing phase. Many men who experienced this system were probably reluctant to engage in homosexual activity for fear that doing so would confirm that they were irreparably condemned to a life of sin. If they dared to mention these feelings in confession or to a spiritual director, most often they would have been counseled to pray longer and harder for these to go away.

So in addition to any confusion or shame that Judge was likely to have felt about sexuality as an adolescent and an adult, an additional constraint he encountered was not being able to talk about his sexuality with others. If he did speak to someone confidentially, he may not have received sound advice, since ignorance and prejudice were prevalent. Many people of that era who did have the courage to seek help or advice from a pastoral minister or a religious superior were often met with messages of rejection and condemnation that only increased their sense of self-hatred.

Judge's friends recalled that he attended many AA meetings comprised only of gay and lesbian people, so he would have encountered many peers who were on a similar journey and who had faced similar challenges to self-acceptance. Bob, an AA member who prefers not to use his last name publicly, said that during the 1980s and 1990s, when Judge lived in Manhattan, he was a regular attendee at the Thursday and Sunday meetings of AA that met at St. John's Episcopal Church in Greenwich Village. Although all were welcome to these meetings, they were primarily structured for AA members who were gay or lesbian. Bob recalled that Judge was an active member of this group, sponsoring people and offering his own story to other members. Judge did not wear his Franciscan robe or clerical garb to the meetings, and Bob said that "if you didn't know he was a priest, you'd have never guessed it."[3] Yet some members who did know he was a Franciscan often made the trip uptown to St. Francis of Assisi parish on Sundays to hear him preach at Mass. His homilies offered good spiritual advice that reflected his familiarity with the AA program.

AA would have offered Judge a safe space to speak with others about personal issues that he had not been able to discuss in church circles. A common AA slogan is "You are only as sick as your darkest secrets," meaning that the less one acknowledges or shares a part of one's life, the more that secret keeps him or her in a state of self-torture. AA encourages members to speak honestly about their lives, even (or especially) the parts that they had worked very hard at keeping secret.

John McNeill, a former Jesuit theologian turned psychotherapist,[4] saw Judge professionally during this period of recovery. McNeill recalled the fears and self-doubts that Judge had about himself, particularly concerning his sexuality and the fact that he was officially connected to a church that offered so many negative messages that supported homophobic attitudes. But this struggle with self, in McNeill's opinion, is what made Judge a holy person. "All the strain and pain," the therapist recalled. "At the same time, it was part of his sanctity. To become a saint, you have to suffer. He came the closest to sainthood of anyone I knew."[5]

Similarly, Brendan Fay, a Catholic advocate for lesbian, gay, bisexual, transgender, and queer (LGBTQ) people who was a good friend of Judge's, recalled what a big role self-acceptance played in the priest's recovery: "Within the recovery movement he found a community of people, a safe space where he could be himself for the first time in his life. Slowly and surely, all the things he had hidden or denied about himself were in the open and the real Mychal Judge could find a home for himself. . . . He knew AA brought him back to the place where he could truly be his most honest self."[6]

Judge's honest "self" had two sides to it. He was naturally jovial and gregarious, and he truly loved being with people. But close friends knew he had an intense interior life where he could be very reflective.

"He was always trying to figure out his place in the world," recalled Fr. Fran Di Spigno, OFM, who lived with Judge and assisted him in his varied ministries. "He wrestled with himself and was always struggling to face up to his own demons." These reflective efforts helped him to empathize strongly with people, Di Spigno noted, because they helped him understand the fragility of human life. "He knew personally about brokenness and he knew what it meant to be human. AA helped him be honest with himself."[7]

Fay said, "One of the things people missed about Mychal Judge is that there was a core of sadness or vulnerability in him. He was very in touch with human vulnerability." And being in touch with that core allowed him to help others. "Good ministers have an outsiderness and apartness to them. And he did, more so than anybody else."[8]

AA also acted as a corrective to some of the harmful excesses Catholic culture had instilled in Judge. Instead of living in the clerical role of someone who was strong for everyone else, AA allowed Judge to admit, accept, and celebrate his brokenness. Instead of feeling responsible for everyone else's happiness, AA showed him that, in reality, he could be responsible for only his own happiness. Instead of hiding and despising parts of his identity, AA encouraged self-acceptance and honesty. Along with looking at the world's timeline in the great cosmic calendar of creation and salvation, he could focus on life according to AA's most famous motto: "One day at a time." Judge's journey into sobriety healed many of his internal struggles and strengthened many of his gifts for friendship and connection that had already been so vibrant. He once commented that he felt the founders of AA had helped humankind more than Mother Teresa had.[9]

Perhaps one of the best-known elements of the AA movement is the Serenity Prayer: "God, grant me the serenity to accept the things I cannot change, courage to change the things I can, and wisdom to know the difference. Amen." The prayer sums up the philosophy of AA: humble acceptance, courageous action, awareness of one's limitations and gifts, and dependence on a Higher Power/God.

Judge often shared with people a prayer he had composed that echoes the same spirituality of humility, acceptance, and courage expressed in the Serenity Prayer, but it also includes a bit of Judge's characteristic wit and self-deprecation: "Lord, take me where you want me to go. Let me meet who you want me to meet. Tell me what you want me to say, and keep me out of your way."[10]

The similarities between the two prayers illustrate how much Judge's personal spirituality was influenced by the AA movement.

While Alcoholics Anonymous introduced Judge to a new form of spirituality, this new program did not replace the Franciscan charism of his religious formation. Judge remained very much a Franciscan, even while he added the new layer of AA spirituality to his life. It was congruent with Franciscan ideals, and perhaps there was no stronger connection between the two than the Franciscan emphasis on Christ's passion, which would have been a strong part of Judge's early formation.

St. Francis saw the cross, with all its pain, suffering, sacrifice, humiliation, and rejection as something to be embraced. It was not to be feared or avoided but welcomed as an authentic way to God and as the most compelling evidence of God's love for humanity. Christ's crucifixion was so essential to St. Francis's understanding of God's love that he became the first recorded person in history to receive the stigmata, the five wounds of Christ, on his own body. The saint embraced this suffering as a great joy.

Similarly, AA emphasized that one should not hide or reject the parts of one's life where pain and suffering existed. Denial is the great enemy of recovery. Denying that one is an alcoholic provides one of the greatest encouragements for the alcoholic to keep on drinking as if nothing were wrong. It's no accident that the main verb of Step 1 is an *admission*.[11] Similarly, denying the existence of pain and suffering in one's life only contributes to continuing to seek alcohol as a way of numbing these feelings. Instead of denying pain and suffering, AA encourages people to admit it.

Father Richard Rohr, OFM, writes that this embrace of the passion is the "unique Franciscan view of the world."[12] Rohr acknowledges that one of the clearest examples of accepting and embracing suffering in the modern world is the 12-Step movement. Indeed, those who have come to terms with their suffering are the ones who become true leaders: "What the crucified has revealed to the world is that the real authority that 'authors' people and changes the world is an inner authority that comes from people who have lost, let go, and are refound on a new level."[13] This passage, a reflection on Franciscan thought, strongly echoes the journey of many 12-Step members: recognizing one has "lost" the struggle by hitting rock bottom, recognizing one's powerlessness, and letting go by handing over control to God, freeing oneself from past mistakes, and achieving a "refound" identity, a more authentic self.

AA gave Judge a new insight into ministry too. The fellowship of AA allowed him to help others but also provided a reciprocal opportunity for him to be ministered to as well. In AA, no person is an ultimate leader or authority. Every person challenges and supports others while at the same time being challenged and supported. Judge thrived in this environment and would carry this dimension of sharing both his brokenness and his gifts into the new ministry opportunities that awaited him. Throughout the remainder of his life, Judge would continue to be a faithful AA member, attending meetings regularly, especially when feeling particularly stressed, and also making himself available for conversation and support to other AA members in between meetings.

Carroll saw that Judge's recovery and acceptance of his whole self made him a more effective minister and church leader. "He was St. Francis on steroids," Carroll observed. "In ministry he emphasized the importance of being yourself, of welcoming others, of being non-judgmental, of accepting people where they were, and always being humble." Judge's own struggle helped him "to look into people's hearts and to see the goodness and humanity there."[14]

A Canterbury Tale

Recovery, however, is not all pain and suffering. The book *Alcoholics Anonymous*—the movement's basic text, sometimes known as "the Big Book" or "AA's Bible"—reads: "We are sure God wants us to be happy, joyous, and free. We cannot subscribe to the belief that this life is a vale of tears, though it once was just that for many of us. But it is clear that we made our own misery. God didn't do it. Avoid then, the deliberate manufacture of misery, but if trouble comes, cheerfully capitalize it as an opportunity to demonstrate His omnipotence."[15]

Seven years after Judge had become involved with AA, he took part in another program that would aid both his recovery, by giving him opportunities to experience, and his practice of the art of living "happy, joyous, and free." In 1985, having completed his assignment at St. Joseph's parish in West Milford, New Jersey, Judge sought permission for a year-long sabbatical program at the Franciscan International Study Centre in Canterbury, England. The program of study and reflection brought together Franciscans from around the English-speaking world for a renewal program for those experienced in living the Franciscan life. During the year that Judge participated in the program, he also celebrated the twenty-fifth anniversary of his ordination.

It is hard to overestimate the significance of this program for Judge. Biographer Michael Ford called it "a watershed" of Judge's life.[16] Judge himself later recalled the experience as "the extraordinary challenging year."[17] Coming as it did at this crossroads in Judge's life, when he was enjoying sobriety and coming to be more accepting of the gift of sexuality, the program was a true renewal for him that would shape the direction of the rest of his life.

From day one, this year would mark a turning point. Judge arrived in Canterbury in the fall of 1985 with long hair (including a small rat-tail braid), an earring, and wearing a denim jacket and jeans rather than his Franciscan robe. While some priests after Vatican II began to grow their hair, rat-tails and earrings were certainly not common. For Judge, though, the change of appearance was not a rejection of his former life as much as it was a new way of living his Franciscan identity. Throughout the year-long program, Judge would discover new dimensions of Franciscan spirituality: joy in life and embracing the countercultural.

Although Judge took courses in Scripture, theology, liturgy, spirituality, morality, and religious culture, it was his extracurricular activities that seemed to be the most liberating for him. He joined an unofficial modern dance class taught by another Franciscan who had once been a part of Paris's famous Folies Bergère music hall. The experience of movement and rhythm helped him become more spontaneous, and it likely fed his burgeoning nonconformist spirit.

Similarly, even though he regularly attended AA meetings in the city of Canterbury, Judge took the unprecedented step of organizing such a meeting at the Franciscan International Study Centre itself. One friar recalled how unusual such a move was: "If a friar had trouble with drink, it was hushed up or he was sent away for therapy. Alcoholism was one of the worst sins." When Judge arrived, openly acknowledging his drinking problem and hosting an open AA meeting right in the friary, he raised more than a few eyebrows.[18]

Perhaps it was being in a new, unrestricted environment that allowed Judge to be more open about his sexual identity too. It is a common dynamic for long-closeted gay and lesbian people to be less self-protective in hiding their sexuality when they are placed in a new geographic location, especially one where traditional expectations about identity are more relaxed. Brian Purfield, a friend from Canterbury, remembered that Judge was indeed more comfortable about discussing sexuality during this year than he had been in the past, though it did not become the focus of his self-presentation to others. "I don't think his sexuality was a big issue for him at that time, but it might have been for other people," Purfield said. "It was intuited or assumed by others. He wouldn't deny his sexuality but he wouldn't promote it either. . . . It was clear he was comfortable with his own life."[19]

In typical fashion for Judge, he often used his self-awareness to help others. A couple of students who were struggling with identity issues found they could talk comfortably with him about their questions. Purfield remembers that the culture within religious communities of the time was that one didn't talk about sexual orientation. But the younger friars "found in Michael someone they could turn to. 'Come on, let's talk about this!' "[20]

Judge talked little about himself in such sessions; as his parish ministry had taught him, he was primarily a listener. As a result, gay friars often assumed he was gay, while heterosexual friars thought of him as straight. For Judge, sexual identity itself was not the problem. The problem, as he had learned from his own experience, was in denying sexuality, a common trap for vowed celibates.

Purfield also recalled a humorous event that poignantly illustrates Judge's priorities. The young friar had noticed that every night Judge would often slip out of his bedroom and disappear somewhere. Curious to see where and with whom Judge might be spending this time, Purfield secretly followed him one evening. He found Judge in the chapel, kneeling, and praying in front of the tabernacle.[21]

The sabbatical year, which was an extension and fulfillment of the work he had begun in AA, helped to liberate dimensions of Judge's personality that had long been dormant or suppressed. In a new setting, he felt the freedom to allow these dimensions to surface. His Franciscan spirit was renewed, allowing him to accept the world as it was created—even the quirks and eccentricities of his own self.

He learned to embrace his sexuality and to develop strong relationships with others.

Judge emerged from AA and the Canterbury experience as a new kind of minister, more like the kind St. Francis had originally imagined for his religious order. Rohr observes that the Franciscan founder hoped his followers would be people "who identified with the poor and the weak and, most especially, their own poverty."[22] This new model of ministry would be characterized by a "new kind of power that looks and feels like total weakness, just as all human suffering and humiliation does."[23] It is a ministry that leads "not from above, and not even from below, but mostly from within, by walking with their brothers and sisters."[24] It is a model that leads ministers to the margins of society. Rohr observes that the "acceptance of growth through suffering is what gives people wisdom and spiritual authority, and finally teaches us love itself—as a gift from beyond."[25]

The AA fellowship gave Judge the opportunity to accept his own suffering, and in the process he discovered an abundance of love. Just as his Franciscan formation led Judge in the direction of institutional church ministry, AA led him out of the institution and toward the lives of all sorts of people living both in and out of the church and Catholic tradition. AA made him a missionary, pushing him beyond the boundaries of the cloister and the church yard. Like a second formation program, it helped him understand how his gifts and his uniqueness could be used to be of service to others.

And when he returned to the United States from Canterbury, it was to the margins that Judge went.

CHAPTER FOUR

On the Margins

New Name, New Ministries

One of the most memorable episodes in the biography of St. Francis of Assisi is the story of his encounter with a man suffering from leprosy. One day Francis was traveling along a road when he saw the man coming toward him. Fear gripped the future saint on seeing this sick man with a dreaded disease. Because people feared contagion, victims of leprosy were ostracized from the community, left to beg and care for themselves as best they could. Against his natural instinct to run, Francis was inspired to approach the man, embrace him, and kiss him. Only later did Francis realize that he had in fact actually embraced and kissed Jesus Christ appearing to him mysteriously in the form of the sick man. The story inspires Franciscans to reach out to the margins, to those excluded from mainstream society, to those who are feared and despised, and to those who have no one to care for them.

Michael Judge returned to the United States from his Canterbury sabbatical renewed in his Franciscan identity and spirituality. Instead of returning to middle-class, suburban parish life, he joined the friary at St. Francis of Assisi Parish in midtown Manhattan—the same parish where young Emmett had first encountered a Franciscan friar and became inspired to join religious life. The move was a return to his roots, but it also found him branching out to areas of ministry that were on the church's cutting edge, embracing and kissing the "lepers" of the twentieth century.

Almost as an omen that new things were about to happen, soon after arriving at 31st Street, he changed his name again, this time from *Michael* to *Mychal*. Keeping a form of *Michael* kept him connected to his father and also maintained part of the name he received after entering religious life, Fallon Michael. One explanation for the change was that it distinguished him from the other men named Michael in the large friary. Yet the pronunciation of both names is the same, so the change of spelling would not have been much of a distinction. He could have also distinguished himself by using *Fallon*, the first part of his religious name. Another explanation was that the change honored his Irish heritage. Yet, the authentic Irish spelling would have been *Mícheál*, so that might not have been the whole reason for the change. Judge remained coy about the shift, suggesting somewhat jokingly that the name choice was inspired by a professional basketball player, Mychal Thompson.[1]

While the choice of *Mychal* is not definitively known, it is significant that he changed his name at all. A change of names fits a common pattern for many gay men, especially of that era, who, after coming to terms with their sexual identity, select a new way by which they will be known. The emotional impact of self-acceptance is often so profound, a sort of rebirth, that adopting a new identifier feels appropriate. While rare that these men will change their name legally, they sometimes opt to be known by their middle name or by their formal first name instead of a nickname (*Robert* instead of *Bob*). The name change signals their new outlook on life and the acceptance of a new, more authentic identity. St. Francis was an urban ministry center, very different from the suburban parishes where Judge had previously served. With few residences nearby, the worshiping community tended to be constantly in flux: out-of-town visitors, workers from the local offices, shoppers from the local stores. On Sundays, people would come for Eucharist from all over the New York metropolitan area, many seeking to pray in a Franciscan church or because they had personal connections with this historic parish or the friars. In a real sense, the parish had no boundaries, and its ministry was directed to the city as a whole. Judge, who thrived on the cacophony and characters of New York City, could not have been more at home. He was back in the Big Apple, where, despite the pollution, at least his soul breathed free.

Judge was part of the parish's regular schedule of multiple daily Masses and opportunities for spiritual counseling or the sacrament of reconciliation. He also became involved in one of the ministries that had made the parish well known throughout the city: St Francis Breadline was established at the parish in 1930, in response to the destitution so many New Yorkers experienced following the stock market crash the previous year, and it continues to provide sandwiches and other food to homeless people to this day.

Young Emmett Judge had been aware of the homeless population of New York City as a young boy. On his many visits to St. Francis Church as a young boy, he would have seen the people on the breadline and would have witnessed the Franciscans' form of nonjudgmental charity. Once a week, his mother would give him and his sisters each a dime for their own spending pleasure. One day, while walking with his twin sister, Dympna, they were approached by a man seeking handouts. Emmett gave him his dime (an exorbitant sum for a child of that era!), and his sister chided him, saying the man would buy only alcohol. "It doesn't matter. If he needs it, let him have it," Emmett replied, more concerned with doing something charitable for the man in need.[2]

Now as a priest at St. Francis's, Judge regularly handed out sandwiches and coffee, socks and underwear, and he helped organize the free clothing room. He also worked at the other end of this ministry, too, securing donations from across the city. He had an arrangement with a nearby dry-cleaning business to collect unclaimed clothing every week for distribution.

He also became involved in fundraising, a gift he had developed during his time at Siena College, and he was soon well known among many of the city's philanthropists and advocates for the homeless, including those in city government. He also sat on the board of Create, Inc., a nonprofit organization founded by a fellow Franciscan that supported homeless people, alcoholics, drug addicts, senior citizens, and others in dire need.[3]

His gift for personal connection made breadline work into more than a distribution of charity. In one sense, his ministry wasn't to "the homeless," but to John and Mary and Howard and Janet and any of the hundreds of homeless people he would befriend over the years. "He knew the names of all the homeless people who gathered around the Pennsylvania Station neighborhood," recalled his confrere Fr. Hines,[4] just as he had remembered the names of all his parishioners in New Jersey. On his frequent walks around Manhattan in his brown friar's robes, Judge was often approached for a handout. He carried a stack of one-dollar bills to distribute to any and all who asked for money. And he made friends out of these anonymous faces.

Salvatore Sapienza was a young Marist brother in the 1980s when he was befriended by Judge and began to assist him in his ministries. Sapienza remembers walking with Judge in the city on an errand when they encountered two homeless men. Judge greeted them as long-lost friends and suggested that they all go to lunch (his treat) at a nearby fast food restaurant. When they sat down to eat, Judge began the conversation with "Such a beautiful night, isn't it?"

Later that same evening, Sapienza accompanied Judge to a fundraiser that was being held in the ballroom of one of Manhattan's elegant hotels. The celebrity guests of honor were the movie star Christopher Reeve and the television actress Marlo Thomas. After Judge was introduced to the celebrities, his conversation opener with them was "Such a beautiful night, isn't it?"

The repetition of this line underscored for Sapienza something that he had already noticed about Judge: the Franciscan approached all people with equal levels of respect and dignity. He made no distinction between social or economic status.[5] In fact, Franciscan spirituality revels in the gospel admonition that "the first shall be last and the last shall be first" (Matt 20:16) and all the topsy-turvy inversions that can occur when that maxim is applied to real life.

Judge spent every Christmas Eve with homeless people. His tradition was to preside at Mass at A Dwelling Place, a Times Square-area shelter run by nuns for women who were homeless or mentally ill. His Franciscan love of making the Incarnation tangible and visible for people meant that he would bring a small doll to the shelter to represent the infant Jesus. He would cradle the doll as he walked up the avenue on Christmas Eve, and when he arrived at the shelter, he would place the doll on the altar and invite the residents and sisters to approach the image to say a little prayer.[6]

A Different Type of Homelessness

During this period, Mychal also became more actively and personally involved with a group of people experiencing a different type of homelessness. Every Sunday in Manhattan, a group of lesbian, gay, bisexual, and transgender (LGBT) Catholics and their supporters met to celebrate Mass together.[7] The Mass was hosted by Dignity/New York, a chapter of the national organization DignityUSA, which had been founded in 1969 by a group of gay and lesbian people under the direction of a California priest, Fr. Pat Nidorf. Most Dignity chapters across the United States had the support of the local diocese or at least the parish where they met, though they were often relegated to church basements or other out-of-the-way rooms.

At the time, many LGBT people were not welcomed in their home parishes. Sometimes they received cold shoulders from parishioners or were explicitly excluded from church activities and liturgies by pastors. This rejection mirrored similar rejections they may have experienced from families, friends, employers, and landlords. The gay liberation movement had made few inroads in society by the mid-1980s, so many LGBT people frequently lived with varying degrees of shame, alienation, and well-founded fears of rejection and even violence. Unfortunately, the way many Catholics understood the church's teaching about homosexuality often encouraged discriminatory attitudes and behaviors against LGBT people.

Official church documents by this time had recognized that a homosexual orientation is not, in itself, sinful. In a

1975 document on sexual ethics, the Vatican's Congregation for the Doctrine of the Faith rejected the idea that homosexuality was a choice by explaining that some people were homosexual because of "some kind of innate instinct."[8] Because a homosexual orientation is not chosen, it is not sinful. In church teaching, one can sin only by carrying out an action that is freely chosen.

Further documents from individual bishops and national bishops' conferences called for respect for lesbian and gay people by including them in parish communities and providing them with pastoral care. The teaching on respect flows from the Catholic social justice principle that all human beings have inherent dignity, share a fundamental equality, and must be respected regardless of any identity characteristic or even behavior. Some church documents condemned prejudice and discrimination against sexual minorities, a notable one even teaching that "prejudice against homosexuals is a greater infringement of the norm of Christian morality than is homosexual . . . activity."[9]

But the church's social justice approach to homosexuality was only a whisper compared to the booming message about sexual ethics. For many decades, church leaders were reluctant to preach the teaching of respect and inclusion, either because they were uncomfortable with the topic or out of fear that people would presume they were endorsing homosexual activity and sexual relationships. For the great majority of Catholics at the time, the scales tipped heavily toward condemnation. The church's rejection of homosexual relationships helped reinforce cultural prejudices and stereotypes about gay and lesbian people.

Of course, there were exceptions to these prevailing Catholic attitudes. A small handful of Catholic voices pushed against the predominant Catholic negativity and silence, emphasizing the church's teaching on respect for all and encouraging church officials to listen to the lives and spiritual journeys of this marginalized population. In addition to Dignity, another group, New Ways Ministry, was founded by Sister Jeannine Gramick and Father Robert Nugent to promote education about the experiences of gay and lesbian people and to encourage respect and pastoral care for this community. For this time period, Judge's outreach to LGBT people "was a very brave thing to do," noted Sapienza. "He wanted to uplift gay people as deserving of dignity and rights."[10] Judge told Sapienza that gay people needed to be embraced and if the church wasn't going to do it, he was.

Judge had been involved with Dignity before his Canterbury experience, but upon his return, he became more deeply involved in this somewhat "underground" ministry. He began to attend the weekly Dignity Mass at St. Francis Xavier Parish in Manhattan and joined a gay priests' support group there. More than occasionally, he presided at Mass for the group. Of course, Judge's natural instinct for ministry and listening often found him in pastoral counseling sessions with members who were having difficulties with coming out, personal rejection, and understanding whether God loved them or not. He was of particular help to Dignity members who were part of the AA movement. While this ministry was deeply personal for him, it was not one that was explicitly accepted by the official church.

At the time, Judge was taking a personal and ecclesial risk by ministering to LGBT people. Even heterosexually oriented ministers who did outreach to sexual and gender minorities risked invoking suspicion about their identity, resulting in marginalization from church circles for their associations with this community. While Judge did not make a public declaration of his orientation, friends said he did selectively come out to those close to him. One of them, Brendan Fay, explained: "Of course, as a Catholic priest, he could not come out publicly, but he was out with whomever he could trust or he thought it would help."[11]

Judge's role allowed him to show a compassionate face of the church to the LGBT community during a period when few other church leaders did so. Just as he "walked a fine line" about his orientation, as one friend put it,[12] he also walked a fine line when it came to becoming involved with more controversial political issues concerning LGBT people. When the New York City Council held hearings about a sexual orientation nondiscrimination bill, Fr. Bernárd Lynch, SMA, who had also been involved in LGBT ministry, was the sole Catholic priest who testified for its passage. Sister Jeannine Gramick of New Ways Ministry was the sole nun who testified. Judge refrained from doing so, but Lynch recalled that Judge had tears in his eyes when he told him, "Bernárd, I admire you. I cannot go with you. But I will support you."[13]

Judge walked the same fine line when it came to ecclesiastical issues. In 1986 the Vatican's Congregation for the Doctrine of the Faith issued its "Letter to the Bishops on the Pastoral Care of Homosexual Persons." This document introduced into church discourse the term "objective disorder" to describe a homosexual orientation, and it referred to lesbian and gay sexual activity as always "an intrinsic moral evil."[14] In addition to this terminology, which many church leaders have called pastorally harmful, the document suggested that lesbian and gay people's relationships were partly responsible for the violence directed against them.[15] Unsurprisingly, the document was widely and strongly criticized by the LGBT community, who saw very little in it that could possibly be called "pastoral care."

The Vatican's letter caused much discussion in the Catholic community, though strong critiques of it were few. Fr. John McNeill, a Jesuit theologian and psychotherapist who had for ten years been silenced under the vow of obedience by his order from speaking on homosexuality, broke this imposed sanction to speak out about the destructive pastoral, psychological, and personal harm the letter's language and recommendations would cause to lesbian and gay people. His public criticism led directly to his expulsion from the Jesuit order. When Fr. Lynch supported McNeill's evaluation, Lynch's community ordered him to a year-long "sabbatical" in Rome, which felt to him more like a punishment than a relaxing and renewing hiatus.[16]

Because the letter recommended that dioceses not allow church property to be used except by groups who explicitly supported Catholic doctrine on sexual ethics,[17] bishops began expelling Dignity chapters across the United States. Though Dignity's mission statement said that gay and lesbian people could "express their sexuality in a manner that is consonant with Christ's teaching," it did not indicate that the group accepted the Catholic Church's teaching that sexual activity between people of the same sex is never permitted. Within a couple of years, almost every Dignity chapter was meeting in Protestant churches for their Catholic services. These expulsions were received by many LGBT Catholics as proof positive that the Catholic Church rejected them. Many simply turned their backs on Catholicism altogether. Even those who remained connected to Catholicism often said they experienced these ecclesiastical decisions as sending them into exile or making them feel as if they were wandering in the desert searching for a spiritual home.

Judge did not speak out against the document. Though friends recall that he privately disagreed with its language and recommendations, he chose not to publicly challenge the church's authority. Lynch explained Judge's decision not to comment on the letter by recalling that Judge saw the church both as an institution and also as the people of God. The Franciscan would not criticize the institution, but he saw his role as being a "people's priest," serving where he could and ministering to others even if that meant going outside of the church's self-imposed borders to do so. Judge told friends that he could not understand the doctrinal position against loving lesbian and gay relationships, and he often observed, "Is there so much love in the world that we can afford to discriminate against any kind of love?"[18]

Standing with People in Hell

While publicly quiet about the Vatican letter, Judge did work to help repair some of the damage that it caused to LGBT people—and in doing so, he became involved in a whole new area of marginalized ministry. When the New York Dignity chapter was expelled from St. Francis Xavier parish, the chapter's ministry to people with HIV/AIDS was under threat of having to close. It was one of only a few Catholic HIV/AIDS ministries operative in New York City at the time.

Judge solved the meeting place problem by welcoming the ministry's gatherings and activities to his own parish, St. Francis of Assisi. He felt it was an important witness that this ministry be housed and conducted in a Catholic institution. With the church doing so little at the time to respond to the AIDS pandemic, maintaining a Catholic identity for the ministry was essential—probably more for the church's reputation than for the people who were served. Liturgies, discussions, counseling, and retreats, all took place in this new Catholic home. While it was Judge's invitation and facilitation that brought the ministry to the parish, it must be remembered that since the Franciscan parish was communal property, it meant that the other friars of his community supported his offer of hospitality too.

This small step inspired Judge to become more involved with those infected and affected by the disease. Since demographically, the syndrome largely affected gay men and intravenous drug users, this new involvement was a natural extension of his ministries with the LGBT community, people with addictions, and people living on the street. AIDS had been identified by the medical profession in 1981, but by the mid-1980s it had already spread widely, having gone undetected in many people for several years previous. Paranoia ran wild since it was still unknown how the virus was contracted. One wild rumor was that the virus might be spread by mosquito bites. Another was that it might be transmitted through sweat, causing some to develop paranoid fears of riding in packed subway cars and buses. Some churches began discontinuing distribution of Communion from the chalice for fear that the sacred cup would spread the contagion.

People with HIV/AIDS were shunned by family, friends, coworkers, and, most sadly, the church. Some hospitals refused to admit people with the virus, and if they did, some hospital workers avoided the rooms of HIV/AIDS patients. Funeral directors refused to prepare their corpses. Some churches denied burial services. For someone to choose to work intimately with this population required the faith and courage of the saint who kissed the leper. It meant experiencing stigma and ridicule in the name of compassion.

Judge tested the water of this ministry with regular visits to Edward Lynch, a friend from AA meetings who was dying from AIDS. Willing to break a rule in the name of compassion, Judge, against visiting policy, would sneak Lynch's favorite foods to his hospital room. When Lynch died, Judge presided at his funeral Mass at St. Francis of Assisi Church. As was common at such events, one side of the church was filled with friends from the AA and gay communities. The other side, with family members and other friends, was much less populated.

At one point during the liturgy, sensing the division among the congregants, Judge asked for people in the pews to offer reminiscences of the deceased. The stories of friendship and support from Lynch's AA and gay friends astounded the grieving family, and after the Mass, the two divided groups merged into one, supporting and comforting one another. Father Michael Carnevale, OFM, the pastor of St. Francis Parish, witnessed this minor miracle and afterward suggested to Judge that he begin regularly ministering to the HIV/AIDS community.[19]

Judge did so by going the next day to the chaplaincy office at St. Clare's Hospital, Manhattan. Despite so much fear of AIDS on the part of the religious and medical establishments, this hospital run by the Alleghany Franciscan Sisters had established one of the first AIDS wards in the city.[20] Sister Pascal Conorti, the head chaplain, recalled that she quickly sensed that Judge intuitively knew how to minister to this stigmatized and suffering population. "I felt in some ways he knew more than I did," she recalled. "Whatever that mind of ours does to put everything in columns—this is good, this is bad—he didn't need to do that. There was sort of a breadth about him that just embraced whoever was there."[21] In his journal that evening, Judge wrote: "I felt on the train home, 'I am at peace today finally. . . . This is what You want me to do. . . . Thank you, Lord.' "[22]

When encountering people who were exhausted, ill, wracked with pain, ostracized from mainstream society, and quickly approaching certain death, what is an effective pastoral response? Judge did what he did best: he listened, reminded them of God's love, and remained a dependable and friendly presence. One friend, Ted Patterson, remembered that Judge approached each patient as if he were making a social visit under ordinary circumstances. "He would just go in and say hello and they would talk to him like crazy. He said, 'God's watching over you and I'm going to bless you and everything is going to be just fine.' He never said you have to be Catholic. He said you have to love yourself and you have to love God. When he left, they'd have a big smile on their faces. They all died happier."[23]

John McNeill recalled that Judge shared with him the approach he took when visiting AIDS patients who were often in seemingly hopeless situations: "He used to put it to me, if you descend into somebody else's private hell and stand there with them, it ceases to be hell. That's exactly what he did. He would go into their pain and rage and sorrow and share it with them and both of them would be blessed by that sharing and feel God's grace and presence. He would go away as fulfilled as the AIDS person he visited."[24]

As in so much of his ministry, Judge did not go it alone but enjoyed being part of a team. He sought ministry partners by placing a classified ad in *Outweek*, a New York City gay news publication. Above a drawing of St. Francis with the New York City skyline in the background, it said, "IN THE SPIRIT OF ST. FRANCIS OF ASSISI . . . serving our brothers and sisters affected by AIDS," followed by the address and phone number of the newly christened "St. Francis AIDS Ministry." One of the handful of people who responded was the Marist brother Salvatore Sapienza, who had already been working with secular HIV/AIDS organizations. He was grateful for the opportunity to work with Judge's Catholic-identified ministry, as a sign that the church as an institution could respond helpfully to the epidemic. When he arrived at St. Francis Parish to meet Judge and join the fledgling ministry, the Franciscan told the young brother, "If Jesus were alive today, this type of work is what He would be doing."[25]

The St. Francis HIV/AIDS ministry would never grow larger than five people: Mychal Judge, Sapienza, two Franciscan friars, and a layman. Sapienza recalled that Judge, who was the oldest of the group, often spent time offering encouragement to this small band of twenty-somethings. At the outset, the younger team members were worried that they would not know what to say during pastoral visits. Judge advised them, "God will give you words to say. If not, then just be silent."[26]

One of the first tasks Judge assigned Sapienza was to lead a prayer service and discussion for HIV/AIDS patients. The young brother did not feel prepared for the task and asked Judge to accompany him. Judge said that he was unavailable. Tentatively, Sapienza agreed, and he surprised himself as an effective leader. As he led the event, he noticed Judge standing in the doorway looking into the room. Later, Judge confessed that he had been available, but he'd declined Sapienza's request for assistance because he wanted the younger brother to muster confidence and leadership. The incident highlighted another of Judge's qualities: "Mychal didn't want to be the focus of the ministry," Sapienza recalled. "He didn't want it to be all about him."[27]

Judge ministered to Sapienza in a more personal way. A few years into working with the HIV/AIDS ministry, the young brother began to question his religious vocation. He had been aware of his gay identity before joining religious life, and he had been happy to choose celibacy as a lifestyle. However, something changed in his life: he had fallen in love with someone. During a retreat for the HIV/AIDS ministry team, Sapienza took a walk with Judge and sheepishly acknowledged that he was in love. Judge's response surprised him: "Oh, I'm so happy for you! I'm so happy you are experiencing love. I fall in love all the time."

Sapienza had been expecting a sterner and more cautionary response, especially since he knew that Judge took his vow of celibacy very seriously. Judge's advice helped Sapienza see that love is an opportunity, not a problem. "God made us to love," Judge counseled him. "Always give gratitude for that gift." Sapienza said that Judge advised him to pray to God, asking that the Almighty would "make this new relationship into what God wanted it to be, not what you want it to be."[28] Sapienza recalls that Judge helped him see his sexual orientation and capacity to love as gifts from God that should be celebrated.

As the pandemic spread and both public apathy and public fear grew, Judge's work began to multiply. His appointment book was filled with hospital visits and funerals. He organized AIDS retreats, attended workshops and support groups, and continued using his personal charm to raise funds for patients' necessities and to raise awareness of the disease and its victims among the influential people he knew.

Judge's compassion and creativity nourished his pastoral ministry. He sometimes massaged the feet of patients he visited with aromatic oils. In addition to offering physical comfort, the gentle gesture went a long way toward softening some hard feelings that some people had about the presence of a priest.[29] He infused his anointing oils with street-bought essential oils to make the sacramental experience more fragrant for those who, near to death, were fading in consciousness. At times, when the pastoral context seemed to call for it, he broke into prayerful, comforting song.

One night, he received a call at the friary from someone looking for "the priest who did AIDS funerals." It was Larry Boies, who was providing full-time care for his partner of eighteen years, Ron Dalto, who was rapidly approaching death. Though estranged from the church because of the way gay people and AIDS patients had been shunned, Dalto's faith in a loving God was strong, and he longed for the sacrament of anointing. He greatly doubted, however, that any priest would perform the rite for him.

Judge arrived at the couple's home in a midtown loft, finding Dalto lethargic, a living skeleton, propped up in a wheelchair. The priest's gentle touch and warm smile ignited instant rapport with the dying man. He heard Dalto's confession, administered the sacrament of anointing, and gave him a fragment of a communion host, which was all the sick man had the strength to ingest. Judge closed the impromptu service with a most impromptu act. He lifted Dalto's fragile body out of the wheelchair and cradled him in his arms like a child, singing soft songs to him, ending with a kiss on the forehead. Mary Laney, a friend of the couple who witnessed the visit, described it as "about as close to mystical experience as you could ever have."[30]

Less than a week later, Judge led the graveside service at Dalto's funeral. The priest reassured the man's parents that they had raised their son with sound principles and virtues, most evident by the love he shared with Boies. He urged them to take pride in their son's faith, as well as in the courage he showed by enduring such a harrowing trauma. Laney commented on how important it was for Dalto's parents to hear such messages: "This is the first priest I've ever heard tell the parents of a gay boy that you should be proud of him."[31]

"Kissing the Leper"

With all three of the populations he served during this period—homeless people, LGBT individuals, and HIV/AIDS patients—Judge was reaching not only beyond the margins but also beyond the comfort zones of most ministers of the time. His own personal struggles prepared him for reaching out to others whose life situations caused them to experience not only physical and emotional suffering but intense shame too. His friend Brian Carroll remarked that this was Judge's great gift in ministry: "He took away the shame. For some people, sexuality is a part of their shame. Or homelessness is a part of their shame. Or addiction is a part of their shame. Mychal helped people embrace all the shame parts of themselves and turn them into something good."[32]

This approach to ministering to these marginalized groups was thoroughly Franciscan. It is easy to recognize Judge's attitude toward ministry in the vision of human beings expressed in the action of St. Francis of Assisi. As one spiritual writer describes the saint's vision: "First of all, he recognized their humanity, not through words, but through actions. He embraced them. Kissed them. Looked them in the eye. He transcended, rather than destroyed, the 'leper' label. In other words, Francis didn't ask us to ignore identities; he asked us to look beyond them. He acknowledged that these men and women were first and foremost children of God."[33]

In his involvement with these ministries, which related to three major social issues of the day, Judge was becoming sewn into the fabric of New York City life. He would become an even greater part of the city's immense tapestry when the health of one of Judge's Franciscan confreres failed, and Mychal was asked to take on another unique ministry.

CHAPTER FIVE

Learning from the Firefighters

Witnessing the Grace of God

"He knew exactly what could happen to him and he went into that building anyway on the chance he could help somebody he didn't know."[1]

Those words perfectly describe the Father Mychal Judge who entered the North Tower of the burning World Trade Center on September 11, 2001. But that sentence was not spoken *about* Mychal Judge. It was spoken *by* Mychal Judge a decade *before* his own death, and he was talking about Kevin Kane, a thirty-one-year-old firefighter who had died after sustaining burns to over 80 percent of his body as he worked selflessly to help extinguish a fire at a Brooklyn building. Judge was at the hospital when Kane died on September 13, 1991, pastorally accompanying the young man, his family, and colleagues. Judge was only a part-time fire department chaplain at the time, not yet sure that he was called to this ministry. In fact, this ad hoc role was something that he stumbled into rather than sought.

New York City Fire Department Engine 1/Ladder 24 is directly across West 31st Street from St. Francis of Assisi

Parish, where Judge lived and ministered in the 1980s and 1990s. It was a unit with many elite-trained firefighters, so it was called on for every large blaze in Manhattan.

Throughout the 1980s, Fr. Julian Deeken, OFM, one of Judge's confreres in the friary, used Engine 1/Ladder 24 as his home base in his ministry as chaplain to New York City's firefighters. One reason the work was important was that the overwhelming majority of New York City's 11,400 firefighters were Catholic (many of Irish descent). Not long before Deeken's death from cancer in 1991, he asked Judge to take over his fire department ministry. Judge hesitated, not sure that he was the right person for the job. He already had more than enough to do with the demands of parish work and his ministry to the homeless, those with HIV/AIDS, LGBT Catholics, and the AA community. After much cajoling, he was persuaded to temporarily help out. In his ministerial life, Judge had become accustomed to being with people in dramatic situations, people living on the thin edge of a razor. And his lifelong love of sirens, excitement, and energy may have partly persuaded him to accept the invitation. He became an associate chaplain for the fire department, filling in part time, but not permanently assigned.

Brian Mulheren, a police officer known as the "night mayor" because he was the designated city official to show up whenever a catastrophe occurred, had been a friend of Judge's since the priest's return to New York. For two years, he pestered the priest to take the chaplaincy job full time. Mulheren remembers telling Judge, "The fire department is the largest parish there is. They need somebody. I kept saying to him, 'You're the person.' "[2] Judge continued turning the offer down, feeling that this ministry would not be a good permanent fit for him.

While at the hospital with Kane's family and fellow fire-fighters, Judge heard Kane's father, Edward, a retired New York City fire chief, encourage the other firefighters to honor Kevin by continuing to do their job, no matter the cost. Witnessing their resolve, Judge was convinced that he was seeing the grace of God in action. He was deeply moved by Kane's sacrifice and the willingness of the other firefighters to continue bravely despite such enormous all-too-apparent risks: "He knew exactly what could happen to him and he went into that building anyway on the chance he could help somebody he didn't know," Judge said of the young man. Reflecting on this selfless attitude, Judge had a simple answer for what motivated these men to risk their lives to save others: it was "the grace of God."[3]

Soon after Kane's death, Judge finally told Mulheren, "Yes."

A New Kind of Parish

Judge's full-time ministry as fire department chaplain began in 1994, serving all the fire stations in Manhattan, The Bronx, and Staten Island. "Full-time" is an understatement because the job meant that Judge was on call 24/7/365, and with a key fire station right across the street, Judge would often know immediately when firefighters were responding to a blaze.

What does a fire department chaplain do? Deeken had explained the job to him this way: "You go to third alarms and just stand there and bless them. Go to the hospitals occasionally. That's all you have to do. It's a very simple job."[4] But Judge would quickly learn that the job was a lot more than just chasing sirens. Although he would never be called to pick up a hose or charge into a blazing building,

Judge had to become like a firefighter by immersing himself in their life and culture—a culture of camaraderie, selflessness, and an amazing degree of unpretentiousness and self-effacement. It was not a far stretch for Judge.

Judge became a regular presence around the city's fire stations, getting to know the men and women he was serving. Fire stations are communities, with personnel living together for two- and three-day shifts, eating, working, relaxing. Judge's natural gift for friendship made this part of the ministry easy, as did his ability to be an attentive, sensitive listener. Through daily life with the firefighters, as well as experiencing life-and-death rescue situations with them, he came to know the people he ministered to much better than he could have known the people in his other ministries.

One important aspect of the ministry was to provide comfort and courage to firefighters at blazes. Lieutenant David Fullam of Ladder 24 firehouse remembers that he and Judge were "probies"—fire department slang for new employees who had to put in a probationary period before being accepted permanently on the force—together. Fullam said he felt secure when he arrived at a fire and saw, amid all the orchestrated chaos of the rescue team, that Judge was there, quietly praying. Judge told Fullam and his friends, "When you come to work, when you step on your rig, you're in a state of grace. You don't have to worry about anything."[5]

Firefighter Joe Falco told *New York* magazine reporter Jennifer Senior, "I would break his chops constantly. I wouldn't treat him like a priest. I'd treat him like any other guy. It wasn't a priest-parishioner relationship. It was . . . you know, man to man. He'd help guys out with their marital problems. With every problem, big or small. You could go to him."[6]

Because of the nature of the work, firefighters' lives contain stressful, emotional situations that are as challenging to face as charging into a burning building. So Judge extended his ministry past the firefighters to their families, whose lives were intimately connected to and intensely affected by a firefighter's unusual work schedule, often not being home several days a week on a regular basis. Their erratic schedules make their home lives complex, with strain on marriage and family relationships a common occupational hazard.

Spiritual counseling was a big part of Judge's ministry. In addition to their unusual family situations, the precarious nature of firefighters' work put them in harm's way far more frequently than most other people. No one could be unaffected by such close familiarity with vulnerability and loss. Sooner or later, all firefighters would have the experience of a comrade being seriously wounded, permanently handicapped, or dead, or would be in just such a situation themselves. The job of a fire department chaplain means being with people as they face life's greatest tragedies.

One of the places where Judge spent a lion's share of his time was at hospitals, at the bedsides of injured and dying firefighters and offering solidarity and comfort to family members, friends, and other firefighters who were a constant presence at these scenes. Fullam remembers accompanying Judge to a number of hospital rooms to be with a comrade who was injured. Judge often stayed through the night—and that could happen night after night after night. Fullam remembers that Judge was often exhausted during these times, but he would stay as long as the firefighter, the family, or anyone needed him there to pray with them.

In one perilous fire, Fullam found himself hanging from a fire escape and had to jump to the ground. Because of injuries he incurred, he was sent to the emergency room, and Judge sat with him while he waited for care. Judge apologized repeatedly to him that he did not have what he usually brought to the hospital immediately following a fire: pairs of dry socks so that the firefighters' feet could be warm and dry.

The Closest Thing to God on Earth

One of the most serious of these hospital visits occurred March 28, 1994, during Holy Week, when several firefighters were severely burned and injured trying to rescue residents of a small Greenwich Village apartment building. What began as a small fire, the result of a resident placing a pizza box on top of a gas stove and leaving the apartment, quickly developed into a deadly blaze. Captain John Drennan, James Young, and Chris Siedenburgh had charged up a staircase to the second floor, as the other firefighters broke through the door of the apartment below where the fire began. The open door allowed fresh air to rush into the room, providing new oxygen for the fire to consume and igniting pent-up gases in the apartment. The result was a fireball so powerful that soon the second floor was ablaze and the three rescuers there were trapped.

When the fire was under control, another team of rescuers entered the building to recover their colleagues and found three bodies on the second floor. Young had been so badly burned that they could barely make out his uniform because it was charred almost beyond recognition. They whisked the barely alive Drennan, a forty-nine-year-old seasoned rescuer, and Siedenburgh, a twenty-five-year-old with less than three years of experience on the job, to New York Hospital-Cornell Medical Center, which housed the city's primary burn unit. The flesh on both men had been scorched intensely. Upon arriving, the barely conscious Drennan's first words were, "Where's Chris? How is he? How is he?" Judge arrived and anointed both men.[7]

Siedenburgh died the next day. Drennan hung on, his wife, Vina, by his side every day. And by her side every day was Fr. Mychal Judge. Judge also ministered to and consoled the constant flow of visitors who came to Drennan's bedside, including major New York City brass such as Mayor Rudolph Giuliani and Fire Commissioner Howard Safir.

For many years, the city had been slow in purchasing bunker gear, a form of highly effective protective garments, for the fire department. Such gear could have prevented, or at least lessened, these three firefighters' injuries. When Abe Lackman, the city's budget director, visited the hospital, Judge took Lackman aside and told him in painful details about the human suffering that the lack of the gear caused. He spoke of the bravery and heroism of the firefighters who courageously risked their lives, even without the protective gear, to rescue people. In short, there was no excuse for not purchasing the equipment immediately. According to Lackman, he left the hospital, returned to his office, and told the mayor that he would find $12 million in the city's budget to buy the gear.[8]

Before this tragedy, Judge had never met Drennan. Vina was Lutheran, and while Drennan had been raised Catholic, he had become a member of his wife's church. Neither his unfamiliarity with Drennan nor the denominational difference mattered to Judge, who stayed at the hospital with Drennan's wife, four children, other family, and fellow firefighters for forty days. On the fortieth day, after surviving several surgeries, fighting off constant infections, and battling organ failure, Drennan died quietly.

Cardinal John O'Connor of New York offered St. Patrick's Cathedral to the Drennan family for the funeral. Vina accepted but said that she wanted Fr. Mychal Judge to preside at the liturgy, rather than the cardinal, whom she did not know. Judge presided and preached at the funeral Mass at St. Patrick's, where an honor guard of five thousand firefighters lined the funeral procession, tears streaming down the faces of even the toughest among them.

For the rest of his life, Judge stayed in frequent contact with Vina, who became a frequent speaker on fire prevention and better safety measures for firefighters. Vina later reflected on the role that Judge had played during this crucial time in the Drennan family's life: "In 40 days he was always there. And when he prayed over John's burned body, you felt you had a chance that God would listen, anyway. You felt that the words were just flying right up."[9]

In a separate interview Vina recalled, "There was always a presence of God in him, a peacefulness in the midst of fear, pain, and suffering. He had that gift of presence."[10]

The fire department's calendar is not merciful. Soon after John Drennan's funeral, another firefighter fell. Lieutenant George Lener of Ladder Company 6 died while searching for survivors in an arson fire at a warehouse in Manhattan's Chinatown. Though he was not breathing when found, he was able to be resuscitated, but he remained comatose. Judge kept vigil with Lener's family at the hospital every day, as he had done with the Drennans. Lener died forty-five days after the fire.

Judge went via helicopter from the hospital to Staten Island with Lener's wife, Maura, to inform the couple's children of their father's death. A few days later, he presided again at a St. Patrick's Cathedral funeral Mass, complete with fire department honor guard. "He was the closest thing you could find to God on earth," Maura said, reflecting on Judge and his ministry to her and her family.[11]

A Theology of Firefighting

Firefighters' near-constant awareness of life and death often inspires them to ask the big, ultimate questions about existence and eternity more than other people do. Firefighters always put others' lives and safety before their own. They trust and rely on one another as deeply as police officers and military personnel do. And because they are ready for this life of service every day, this faith in each other becomes background for them, something not necessary to talk about, but simply to live. Though firefighters may be the last to admit it, firefighting has a sacred dimension to it.

"Firefighters ask me to bless them, but I feel blessed by them," Judge would say.[12] Far from being a ministerial cliché, this sentiment expressed the fact that as he lived among the firefighters, Judge was experiencing a new kind of spirituality that was more based in actions than ideas or words. On one occasion, he told the firefighters, "The firehouse is a holy place. It will always be holy ground for you."[13]

Firefighters' innate religious sensibility is often channeled into ritual. Judge presided at many ceremonies honoring and remembering those who had fallen in the line of duty. The most common of these events was the raising of plaques at fire stations in memory of the fallen. Judge worked to give these events an extra dimension of respect and mystery. At one of his first memorial Masses, Judge made the event more reverent by providing a gong bell to be rung after each man's name was solemnly heralded. Biographer Daly observed that Judge saw that remembrance was a holy practice for these men: "He understood this was their scripture, the memorialization of all that had come before, that rode with them as they lived one alarm at a time, that came with them into the blinding smoke and searing flame, that would continue no matter what befell them, that would honor for all time those who made the ultimate sacrifice."[14]

Judge knew, too, that despite their innate spirituality, these men were not angels. While he spent many hours praying with them, he also spent a great deal of time at their parties and celebrations, trading jokes, telling stories, and singing songs. "Holy rascals," he would call them. As counselor to them, he knew their human frailties, and he understood these imperfections as he understood his own.

Where There Is Hatred, Let Me Sow Love

Among the firefighters' human frailties was a strain of homophobia that regularly came out in jokes and comments in casual conversations. In the intimate living arrangements of most (predominantly male) firehouses and the strong emotional camaraderie that firefighters shared, some of them became alarmed by any suspicions of homosexuality among their brethren.

At one point, a rumor began to circulate about Judge, not only that he was gay but that he had propositioned one of the firefighters. The rumor collected such steam that Judge had to return from a short vacation to address it. He sought advice from two good friends, Peter Johnson and his son Peter, Jr., who were well connected to New York City government and politics. Asked by them if he had violated his vow of celibacy, Judge answered directly: "No."

The Johnsons arranged a meeting the next day with the leaders of two fire department unions. When asked if he were gay, Judge responded, "Whether I am or not, I never approached anybody."[15] The answer was accepted by the leaders as a warrant to squelch the rumors. Judge's phrasing of the answer also asserted his right to personal privacy and maintained his privilege about with whom he would share this kind of information. The rumors stopped.

His orientation intersected with his fire department chaplaincy in another way too. A rumor circulated that Fire Commissioner Thomas Von Essen was having difficulty accepting one of his sons who had just come out as gay. Judge paid the commissioner a visit, and said to him, "What would you say if I told you I was gay?" Von Essen responded that we would not be surprised, having heard the earlier rumors, but that he realized Judge's orientation would not interfere with his effectiveness as a priest or as a good human being. "I just wanted you to know," Judge responded.[16] Von Essen learned that Judge was someone with whom he could share his concerns and questions about his son.

Though he mostly kept his associations with the gay community private from the firefighters he ministered to, there came a time when Judge felt so comfortable with both worlds in which he lived that he decided to connect them. One year, the fire department's Emerald Society Pipes and Drums corps decided to honor Judge at their annual dinner-dance as one of three "Irishmen of the Year." Over eight hundred people attended, the majority of them being firefighters and fire department officials.

Judge invited his sisters, some AA friends, and a number of fire department friends to sit at the table for his guests. Also included in this group was Brendan Fay and Tom Moulton, a gay couple he knew well. Fay, a native of Ireland, was a very public advocate for LGBT equality, particularly in Catholic and Irish circles. Judge also invited Al Alvarado, a gay man with whom Judge had developed a close relationship. Michael Mulligan, whose deceased gay partner, Stephen Smurr, was one of the first HIV/AIDS patients that Judge ministered to, was also in attendance. Fay recalled feeling a bit uncomfortable during the event, not knowing how public he could be about his identity and relationship with Moulton. Yet, he also marveled at Judge's courage in bridging these two worlds of friends who would otherwise have been mostly at odds with one another.

The high point of the event came when Judge encouraged the guest table attendees to "get up and dance." They did so, forming a dance circle of friendship, a reconciliation of people who might otherwise consider each other as enemies. Following his Franciscan charism, Judge was acting as an instrument of peace, sowing love where there was potential hatred.

The fire chaplaincy overlapped with Judge's other ministries in other ways too. The firefighters knew of his outreach to homeless people and supported him with collections of clothing and money. In regard to this ministry, they also were keenly aware of his penchant for giving away gifts meant for him personally. "If we knew he was going on vacation and we wanted to give him a little spending money, we would put it in an envelope marked 'Do not open until destination' because we knew if he opened it sooner, he would give the money to his homeless friends," Fullam recalled.[17]

Firefighter Carol Walsh said she connected with Fr. Judge because of their shared fellowship in AA. She had first met him in a church vestibule at a firefighter's funeral. He was pacing nervously back and forth.

"I never know what I'm going to say at these things," Judge confessed to her even though they had just met.

"God will speak through you," Walsh told him, an expression that was familiar to Judge from AA meetings.

"Are you a friend of Bill W.'s?" he asked her, referring to one of AA's anonymous founders—the common coded way fellowship members use to identify others in the movement. Walsh acknowledged that she was, and they discussed their journeys and sobriety with one another that day and then further on other occasions. Walsh also attended several of the retreats that Judge led for firefighters who were AA members.

"When he spoke to you, he took you into his confidence," she said. "He made you feel like a friend." Walsh sought

Judge out a few years later when she was planning on divorcing her husband. While she expected she would be lectured about the sanctity of marriage, his simple response to her story was, "Don't stay with someone who is mean to you." Instead of telling her she had a "cross to bear," as she anticipated, he instructed her on the importance of building a relationship based on mutual love.

Walsh had been permanently injured combatting a fire, so she was taken off firefighting duty. Because she had a background in filmmaking, she was assigned to the department's instructional film unit. To transport her bulky equipment, Walsh drove a Jeep Liberty sports utility vehicle. Judge occasionally enlisted Walsh and her vehicle to make deliveries of food and clothing to homeless people and people with HIV/AIDS. On one occasion, he packed the car with over a dozen comforters. When they arrived at a crumbling apartment building in lower Manhattan, she helped him distribute the blankets to each resident of the building, all of whom had HIV/AIDS.[18]

A Second Religious Order

More than being like a parish to Judge, the fire department became a second home. And as much as the lives of the firefighters and their families were touched by his ministry, he, in turn, was changed by their example of self-sacrificing service. Judge had become as close to the firefighters as he had been with his confreres in the Franciscans. In some ways, the two communities were not very different. Each held closely to the belief that all human beings deserve to be saved and that saving them sometimes meant risking one's own life. The Franciscans had taught Judge the importance of faith, the paradox of losing one's life in order to find it, and the importance of communal life. The firefighters embodied these same values in the secular world of safety and lifesaving. The shared credo was "A life is a life and every life is equally worth saving even at the risk of losing your own."[19]

When Judge had a gall bladder attack in the friary, the driver of the ambulance wanted to take him to the closest hospital, St. Vincent's Medical Center in Greenwich Village. He insisted on going instead farther uptown to New York Hospital-Cornell Medical Center, where he had spent many hours and days with injured men and their families. Biographer Michael Daly commented that going to this location was for Judge "a spiritual extension of his other religious order, the FDNY."[20]

The decade that Judge spent with the firefighters taught him a particular kind of courage. It was the kind of courage that motivated him to take on a ministry for which he initially didn't feel competent. It was the kind of courage that motivated him to bridge two communities disposed to be opposed to one another in the hope that some reconciliation and understanding would occur. It was the kind of courage that he had seen practiced scores of times by the firefighters: the courage to rush into a building when everyone else is running out, because you think it is possible to help someone you didn't know.

CHAPTER SIX

Native New Yorker

A Love Affair

Throughout his priesthood and entire life, Fr. Mychal Judge had a love affair. The object of his affection renewed and refreshed him, inspired him and calmed him, provided a reason to get out of bed every morning. Despite the length of his relationship, he was always finding new and exciting things about his heart's desire. The passion of his love never diminished, but, in fact, it seemed to increase with each passing year.

Mychal Judge was in love with New York City.

Having grown up in a highly urban section of Brooklyn, the city was bred in his bones. He loved the buildings, he loved the sidewalks, he loved the subway, he loved the churches, he loved the city's ability to surprise people. He loved its exciting energy, and most of all he loved its people, an amazing bundle of quirky characters, young and old, poor and rich, anonymous faces in the crowds and outstanding celebrities.

During his many years in pastoral work in suburban New Jersey, Judge often returned to his hometown to be reenergized. One of his frequent habits was to walk from Manhattan to Brooklyn, across the Brooklyn Bridge. The Brooklyn Bridge is not just a connector of geography and people. The very architecture of the bridge inspired spirituality. John Roebling, the bridge's architect, had designed the two stone towers, each with two Gothic archways, to evoke cathedral windows. Roebling believed New York needed a soul.

This massive structure connected the two very different worlds of cosmopolitan Manhattan with the neighborhood-oriented borough of Brooklyn. It's a placid spot, above the East River, with a stunning view of the harbor, skyscrapers, factories, warehouses, and homes. It was a place Judge could go to be quiet in the midst of the metropolis's commotion. On the wooden walkway and the barreling roadway full of cars passes the great mass of humanity of New York, people from every background in wondrous diversity. There's probably no better spot in the city to be simultaneously energized by the hubbub and at peace, watching seagulls dip and swoon over the flowing water.

In the 1980s, when he was living in Manhattan, Judge told a reporter, "There is something for me about the Brooklyn Bridge—I must walk it at least once a week. . . . I get ideas on the Brooklyn Bridge even when I'm not looking for one."[1] Just a couple of months before 9/11, Judge had the occasion to walk across the bridge one evening with his friend, Fr. Richard Rohr, OFM, observing the lower Manhattan skyline, dominated by the World Trade Center. Rohr remembered that Judge had "an intuition about the special quality of that place," as if the bridge contained something mysterious and holy. Rohr further recalled their musings on that evening: "We reminisced and theologized about New York. He clearly loved the whole city immensely, its people and its architectural achievements too."[2]

From 1986 until his death in 2001, Judge lived and ministered in the Big Apple, right at the city's very heartbeat in midtown Manhattan, just blocks from the pulse of the ever-energetic Pennsylvania Station, one of the city's main entrance and exit points, active 24/7/365. What to others would be a discordant blare of honks and alarms was to Judge sweet music. While others may have choked on the smoke and the smells that permeated the city's air, Mychal Judge breathed it in deeply. In what is perhaps his most un-Franciscan aspect, Judge felt more at home in urban tumult than he did in nature's serenity.

"I think there's a great sense of God in New York," he told a journalist in 1978. "Across the country, there's land and land and land and land. Yet all the people crowd into the cities. They need the warmth of each other's person. God is there. He keeps them together. I like to walk the streets of New York."[3]

New York City is home to some of the world's most powerful and influential people, as well as some of the most downtrodden and defenseless. While Mychal's primary ministries were with the city's broken and marginalized people, he also became a ministerial presence to some of the city's most well-known and dominant personalities. From church leaders to political figures, Judge had an influence on some of the most important shapers of policy and culture in New York. As a result, in an indirect way, he became one of those shapers himself.

Where There Is Injury, Pardon

Almost immediately after his return to New York at the end of August 1986, Mychal was thrown unexpectedly into the circle of New York City's celebrities. On his second day at St. Francis of Assisi Parish, Judge's confrere Fr. Julian Deeken, the fire department chaplain, asked him to say Mass at Bellevue Hospital for a young police officer who had been recently shot in the line of duty and was paralyzed. Officer Steven McDonald had initially not been expected to live, but he survived the shooting, though unable to move from the neck down. A police chaplain had been regularly saying Mass for McDonald and his family and friends in the hospital room, but on this particular weekend, the priest could not be there. Deeken was asked to be a substitute, but he, too, was also otherwise engaged. He made the request of Judge, who agreed to do so.

While he was well versed in hospital visits by this point in his priesthood, this occasion was very different, because McDonald's injury and touch-and-go recovery had been headline news in the city constantly since he was shot by a teenager on July 12. It had been nearly two months, but Judge had only recently returned from Canterbury so was unaware of the story. The pastoral aspect of the visit proceeded as usual, with Judge's friendliness and humor warming hearts. Yet he would have also noticed that McDonald's hospital room was becoming a focal point for top city and church officials. Also visiting McDonald that night was New York's Cardinal John J. O'Connor.

Besides being Judge's introduction to New York's governing elite, this hospital visit, perhaps more importantly, also served as his introduction to the bravery, faith, and sacrifice of those who served in New York's uniformed services. Ministering to McDonald and his family gave the priest his first insight into what made these courageous men and women tick. Crucially, given the way Judge died fifteen years later, that was also the night Judge was introduced to another city leader visiting McDonald, the police officer Brian Mulheren, who would later convince him to become the fire department's chaplain.

Despite being surrounded by important personalities that night, McDonald and his wife, Patti Ann, were amazed by this priest who ended the hospital room liturgy by breaking into song. Patti Ann asked if he could visit again for Mass, and Judge did so whenever the police chaplain couldn't make it. This visit was the beginning of a years-long close friendship between the McDonalds and Judge. He became a spiritual adviser to them, which included teaching Steven the Prayer of St. Francis, which begins:

Lord, make me an instrument of your peace:
where there is hatred, let me sow love;
where there is injury, pardon.

Six months after the attack on Steven, Patti Ann gave birth to the couple's child, Conor, an event that McDonald described as "a message from God that I should live, and live differently."[4] Soon afterward, McDonald did something that was almost as shocking as being shot: he publicly forgave his attacker. "I forgive him and hope he can find peace and purpose in his life," McDonald said in a public statement. He would later explain the reason for this decision: "I wanted to free myself of all the negative, destructive emotions that this act of violence awoke in me—the anger, the bitterness, the hatred. I needed to free myself of those so I could be free to love my wife and our child and those around us. I often tell people that the only thing worse than a bullet in my spine would have been to nurture revenge in my heart."[5] It was the Prayer of St. Francis made real.

In an interview after Judge's death on 9/11, McDonald credited the priest's pastoral care with enabling him to take this step of forgiveness. He said that Judge "more than any-thing, reaffirmed my faith in God, and that it was important to me to forgive the boy who shot me. And I'm alive today because of that."[6] While Judge was a spiritual counselor for McDonald and his wife, the couple also exemplified for Judge his strong belief that God exists wherever goodness exists, or as he wittily put it (turning the common expression "God is good" upside down), "Good is God."[7]

After months of therapy, McDonald regained the ability to speak, and he began to make public appearances in both the civic and ecclesial circles of the city. From his wheelchair and attached to a breathing machine, the paralyzed officer preached reconciliation, offering his own dramatic story as evidence that even those divided by thick walls of fear, anger, and hatred could become reconciled. Judge, who would phone McDonald every night for a chat during his recovery, frequently joined him at speaking engagements around town. Some saw the pair as a spiritual powerhouse: the Catholic faces of both the NYPD and the FDNY. When Steven was able to travel, Judge joined the couple on a pilgrimage to the Marian shrines of Lourdes, Fatima, and Medjugorje. They also visited Rome, where they met Pope John Paul II at a papal audience.

One place where McDonald preached reconciliation was Northern Ireland, where decades of animosity and bloodshed between Catholics and Protestants had fostered a culture of hate and violence. Judge traveled with the McDonalds on several trips there and helped them organize public demon-strations of reconciliation. Whenever he had a public role at one of these events, Judge would begin by offering the Prayer of St. Francis.

On the occasion of the annual Orange Order march, one of the most controversial displays of Protestant power, McDonald, Judge, and their group of American peacemakers walked down a Catholic-populated street, Garvaghy Road, to the Protestant Drumcree Church, where they greeted the rector, but only after having passed through a series of protestors with weapons who menaced them. McDonald recalled: "I was physically shielded from them so they started to shout at Father Mike. 'We don't allow people like you in here,' they screamed. They were threatening him, and here he was in his priest clothing. But Father Mike just looked at them and smiled. And then he went into the church as planned."[8]

McDonald died in January of 2017, sixteen years after Judge. On his deathbed, his now-adult son Conor placed two items on his father's chest: a copy of the Prayer of St. Francis and a copy of Fr. Mychal Judge's final homily given on September 10, 2001. With family and friends surrounding McDonald's hospital bed, Conor read aloud part of that homily, which spoke of the courage and faith of firefighters, but which could also be said of police officers:

> That's the way it is. Good days. And bad days. Up days. Down days. Sad days. Happy days. But never a boring day on this job. You do what God has called you to do. You show up. You put one foot in front of another. You get on the rig and you go out and you do the job—which is a mystery. And a surprise. You have no idea when you get on that rig. No matter how big the call. No matter how small. You have no idea what God is calling you to. But he needs you. He needs me. He needs all of us.[9]

Judge's friendship with this city hero introduced him to a number of New York City's celebrities. He became an unofficial chaplain to many leaders in city government and the social elite who often sought him out for spiritual and moral counsel. On one occasion, as he was departing

Cornell-New York Medical Center after visiting a wounded firefighter, he learned that Jacqueline Kennedy Onassis was also a patient there. He turned around, found her room, and paid her a pastoral visit.

Mayor David Dinkins and the St. Patrick's Day Parade

One city official he befriended was Mayor David Dinkins, who served in that office from 1990 to 1993, as the city's first African-American mayor. Dinkins and Judge shared a common approach to people and problems: they both tried to be reconcilers. In the years before Dinkins's run for office, there had been a number of high profile, racially charged incidents that dominated the headlines and divided the city. Dinkins campaigned with the message of appreciating New York's diversity, calling the city a "gorgeous mosaic." He vowed to facilitate racial healing, a tall order for a city with so many deep-set ethnic and racial barriers. As fire department chaplain, Judge attended Dinkins's 1990 inauguration at City Hall, an event that celebrated diversity by including, among other things, a benediction by Cardinal John O'Connor and a performance of "New York, New York" by the city's Gay Men's Chorus.

The honeymoon of tolerant diversity did not last long. A new set of highly charged racial incidents erupted under Dinkins's administration, and the mayor's approval rating began to plummet. Judge supported Dinkins's quixotic hope for greater reconciliation, and so he organized a letter-writing campaign among the friars and his friends and hand delivered the supportive missives to City Hall. To thank the friar, Dinkins visited the St. Francis Breadline and met Judge. They shared a cup of coffee afterward, and the two became good friends.

Despite setbacks, Dinkins continued to promote diversity and reconciliation in the city. In 1991, the mayor set himself a herculean task: to resolve a dispute concerning lesbian and gay people marching in New York's St. Patrick's Day Parade. The Irish Lesbian and Gay Organization (ILGO) had applied for a permit to march as a group in the parade but were turned down by the Ancient Order of Hibernians, the event's organizer. Thirty additional groups were already in a waiting list for the parade, the Hibernians said, and they were constrained by the city's time limit for the march. When Dinkins offered to extend the time, the Hibernians told ILGO that their application was submitted late.

Dinkins continued to negotiate, finally brokering a solution that allowed the ILGO members to march in the parade, but only as part of another group's contingent and only as long as they carried no signs or identifying markers. The mayor, who usually has a prized position at the head of the parade, invited ILGO to march along with his contingent, which included the midtown chapter of the Hibernians. The members of ILGO agreed.

The peace, however, did not hold. All along the parade route, they were booed, hollered at, and occasionally showered with beer, including having two cans lobbed at them. When the contingent passed the reviewing stand at 64th Street, all of the Hibernian officials stood and turned their backs toward them. *The New York Times* quoted Dinkins: "It was like marching in Birmingham, Alabama" during the civil rights movement. "I knew there would be deep emotions, but I did not anticipate the cowards in the crowd."[10]

When ILGO was again denied admission to the parade in 1992, Dinkins did something no mayor had done before: he refused to march at all. Judge was at Gracie Mansion, the mayor's residence, on the day of the parade when Dinkins announced his decision. Dinkins's news immediately put Judge in a moral dilemma. As chaplain of the fire department, an organization whose employees were 40 percent of Irish descent and that boasted one of the biggest contingents in the parade, he was expected to march with them. However, he also viewed the denial of ILGO as unjust. Judge decided to march with the firefighters.

When later that morning Judge went to the St. Patrick's Day Mass at the cathedral of the same name, Cardinal O'Connor called on parade participants and spectators to eschew the negative behavior from the previous year. "No one may this day call himself or herself an Irishman, or pretend to be representing the Catholic Church, who treats anyone with contempt or with slander or with violence of any sort," O'Connor said. But he also had an ominous message for the mayor, who was sitting out this parade on a matter of principle. "We will not forget."[11]

At the 1993 St. Patrick's Day Mass, O'Connor, who had always strongly supported the ban against ILGO, offered a stinging rebuke to those who would welcome the lesbian and gay group: "Neither respectability nor political correctness is worth one comma in the Apostles' Creed."[12] Going further, he dedicated the parade to a group of Catholic Irish martyrs of the sixteenth century, casting the dispute as a battle between faithful Catholics and those who had betrayed their faith for politics. Just a few blocks from the cathedral, two hundred peaceful protestors who opposed the ILGO ban were being arrested for sitting on Fifth Avenue's asphalt in a symbolic effort to stop the parade.

While he had been unable to play a role in the St. Patrick's Day Parade dispute, Judge continued to publicly support Dinkins. In 1993, Judge, in his role as HIV/AIDS minister, marched alongside Dinkins, in the city's Gay Pride Parade, passing the same cathedral the Irish march traditionally passed. As testimony to the many roles that he managed, he left that parade early to honor his commitment to be with the firefighters at the department's Emerald Society Pipes and Drums band concert, held in the shadow of the World Trade Center.

The St. Patrick's Day Parade controversy continued year after year, with the ILGO group continually being excluded. In 2000, Catholic gay activist Brendan Fay organized New York City's first inclusive St. Patrick's Day Parade, with the theme of "Cherishing All the Children of the Nation Equally." Judge supported his friend's initiative with encouragement and financial donations, but Fay understood that Judge had made clear in the past that he believed his public position meant that he could not attend such events. So it was a surprise and a delight to Fay when he saw Judge arriving in his Franciscan habit and sandals to march. "He walked along the route as a group of angry protestors, holding up rosary beads and crucifixes, screamed from the sidelines. Mychal just looked at them, smiled, gave them a blessing or waved. He would always say, 'Resentments will do us in.' He lived by that and people saw that. He wasn't angry or resentful in return. He looked on these people more with pity and compassion."[13]

It wasn't until 2015 that the city's St. Patrick's Day Parade allowed an openly LGBTQ group to march with an identifying banner. "Out@NBCUniversal," a group of LGBTQ employees at the NBC television network, which airs the parade, was the first such group allowed to march. In 2016, the Irish-American group Lavender and Green Alliance became the first Irish LGBTQ group to march. Fay continued his inclusive St. Patrick's Day Parade, and perhaps as a testimony to the bridge building that Judge's life and ministry had accomplished, the fire department's Emerald Society Pipes and Drums band led the inclusive parade in 2015.

Cardinal O'Connor

Judge had become a minor Catholic celebrity in New York. Some of his friends teased him that he craved such attention, but his colleague Salvatore Sapienza had a different perspective. Sapienza remembers that wherever Judge went around the city, whether he was talking with politicians, movie stars, homeless people, parishioners, friends, or strangers, he always wore his Franciscan habit and sandals. As a religious brother himself, Sapienza could have also worn a habit but didn't do so because he did not want to stand out. But Judge, he said, *wanted* to look different. Sapienza said Judge wasn't motivated by ego but wore his habit to show people that the Catholic Church was involved in the issues of the day. "He loved being a Franciscan and he loved representing the Church," Sapienza said. "He wanted to show people that being Catholic could be 'cool,' relevant, offering the world an option."[14] He used his minor celebrity status to draw attention to the issues behind the ministries in which he was involved. He liked the idea of speaking truth to power in an inviting way, because he recognized that this is what Jesus did.

One New Yorker with whom Judge had trouble getting along with was Cardinal O'Connor. A conservative churchman who strongly emphasized doctrine and canon law, O'Connor described himself as someone who "could never even be perceived as compromising Catholic teaching."[15] Like Judge, he was also a gregarious man with an affable personality. Yet he was unafraid to speak his mind to city officials and politicians, defending what he saw as attacks on Catholicism and its moral ideals.

The antagonism between O'Connor and Judge never erupted into a public brouhaha, but friends knew of the tense relationship. The exact reason for the disharmony is unknown, but there were several likely factors. For one thing, the ecclesial style of the two men was very different: O'Connor was a traditionalist, whereas Judge favored progressive ideas. More than a few times, Judge had been called into the chancery office because of reports that he had not observed all liturgical rubrics. Where O'Connor enforced rules, Judge was more inclined to bend them based on situational factors and pastoral needs. The two personalities represented two different views of the Catholic identity.

As gay and lesbian issues continued to emerge as political flashpoints in the city, O'Connor and Judge found themselves on different sides of the topic. O'Connor took a very public approach in opposition to initiatives promoting gay and lesbian equality, fearful that these measures undermined Catholic moral teaching. Judge took a more private and pastoral approach to gay and lesbian people, intent on promoting a compassionate face of the church. The one area where they seemed to agree was in the arena of HIV/AIDS. Both were publicly involved in HIV/AIDS work, with O'Connor volunteering at St. Clare's Hospital on a regular basis to help care for patients.

But their mutual dislike stemmed less from their differences and more from their similarities. Both men were sociable personalities and comfortable in the limelight, which perhaps cast too narrow a glow to fit the both of them. Both were proud of their Irish heritage, and both prized their connections with one of New York City's strongest Irish institutions, the FDNY. Both also prized their relationships with public figures, eager to dispense each one's brand of spiritual and policy advice to the city's power brokers.

As head of the archdiocese, O'Connor had the official megaphone to broadcast the city's Catholic voice both inside and outside the church. Judge had no such advantage, yet he still was able to utilize his personality and network of connections to make his Franciscan Catholic voice to be heard by the city's influencers. Throughout their time together in the city, the two men mostly remained at odds with one another.

Mayor Rudy Giuliani and First Lady Hillary Clinton

Judge was with Dinkins at what had been hoped to be a victory party on election night 1993, when the mayor who tried to be a reconciler was defeated for reelection by US prosecutor Rudolph "Rudy" Giuliani, who cultivated a public persona of being "tough on crime." It had to have been disappointing for Judge that the neck-and-neck race was decided primarily by votes from Staten Island, the home of so many firefighters, whose union had backed Giuliani. As concession became apparent, the angry and depressed crowd of supporters in the ballroom began loudly protesting the mayor's decision to concede. Judge stepped in to lead the assembly in prayer, asking them to join hands, still their voices and their hearts, while he offered a blessing to the mayor and this community of supporters.

Dinkins later recalled, "I guess he believed in all people. He certainly believed in me. . . . I considered him one of my best friends."[16]

Giuliani was a man of a different political party, style, and approach to government than Dinkins. He often met Judge at the sites of major fires or other calamities, and the Franciscan became a sort of spiritual counselor to this mayor whose politics were so different from his own. Besides the usual political controversies, Giuliani's administration was also marked by his marital and relationship problems, which had become the talk of the town. When Giuliani was accused in a magazine article of having an extramarital affair, Judge extended his counseling to the person he felt truly needed support in this controversy: Cristyne Lategano, the woman identified in the article. Lategano remembered that Judge had told her, "Don't let them get you down. It'll make you stronger."[17]

After a second affair had become public, Giuliani separated from his wife, whom he eventually divorced. During the time of separation, Judge received frequent phone calls from the mayor to discuss his marital and romance woes.[18] Just as he was available for homeless people, AIDS patients, AA members, and firefighters at all hours of the night, Judge spoke with Giuliani at any time of the day that the mayor needed. As Giuliani was not a religious man, Judge offered him the simple advice, useful for all difficult situations, which he gave to people of all social classes: "Life is complicated. Remember the good things you do. Keep thinking about that. Keep building on that and you'll come to an answer."[19] Instead of focusing on guilt and mistakes, Judge encouraged recognizing God in the positive aspects of one's life.

Judge's connections with public personalities went beyond city officials. Among his friends and fans was Hillary Clinton. The relationship was forged beginning in 1998, as her husband was embroiled in the controversy surrounding his relationship with White House intern Monica Lewinsky. In advance of the annual White House prayer breakfast, White House staff had asked political officials in New York to recommend a clergy person who would sit next to Mrs. Clinton during the event who would have the grace and manner not to allude to her personal marital difficulties, even if only in an indirect way by speaking of forgiveness or moving on after adversity. The name they received was Mychal Judge's.

Judge attended—the date was September 11, 1998—and, true to form, he proved a delightful meal companion for the First Lady, filled with charisma as he gushed very genuinely over the trappings of the executive mansion. Hillary Clinton was charmed by this unusually friendly and down-to-earth clergyman. Her genuine laughter was a surprise to her assistants who had been so worried how this event would transpire. "It was so much fun," she would later recall, mentioning how deeply moved she had been by Judge's outreach to "people overlooked, left out." Mrs. Clinton and Judge met again the following year when both marched together in the inclusive St. Patrick's Day Parade in Queens, New York.[20]

TWA Flight 800

In the early morning of July 18, 1996, Judge received a call from Steven McDonald that TWA Flight 800 from New York to Paris had crashed in the water off Long Island, just outside the city. Recognizing that emergency site chaplains would be needed at this catastrophic human tragedy, in less than an hour Judge was at a hotel near John F. Kennedy International Airport, where shocked and grieving families were gathering to await news of their loved ones. Any news that did arrive was not good.

Judge spent several hours ministering to the families on that visit. He returned to the friary for a few hours of sleep but by midmorning, he was back at the hotel. By this point, it had become apparent there were no survivors. What had begun as a rescue mission now turned into a search for bodies that would continue for sixteen days and produce few results.

While Judge's years of ministry had prepared him for dealing with grief, this situation was starkly different. Unlike the tragedies of the firefighters, the people who died in this event had not chosen to risk themselves for some greater good. Similarly, firefighters' families always know there is a chance of injury and death, but these victims' families were totally unprepared for such a tragedy. And far different from fire deaths, most of these families did not even have the comfort of caring for their loved ones' remains.

These differences caused victims' families to experience a unique and rare kind of pain. On the second day, when Judge appeared at the families' gathering in his habit and sandals, he was confronted by the father of a high school student who had been heading to Paris on a school trip with two dozen of his classmates. The father turned his anger toward Judge: "What are you doing here? What the hell are you doing here? All these people died. You represent God. How can there be a God? How can you believe in God? What God would let all those kids die? It's all a big lie."[21]

Judge responded by holding the man's hand and encouraging him to continue to express his emotions. The man ended up breaking into tears and falling into the priest's arms. The only words Judge could muster were those of his own honest and vulnerable confusion: "God lets evil happen and I don't understand why."[22]

Mayor Giuliani, who was at the hotel and observed Judge's encounter with the suffering father, noticed a simple pattern to the priest's ministry style: "A lot of it is just listening. People are going to get angry. Let them get angry. Let them get it out." The mayor said that he followed Judge's example when speaking with people after 9/11. But the mayor also acknowledged that the priest had a particular gift for this kind of response: "There is no way to exaggerate his ability to understand people and get into their minds and hearts."[23]

The anger, sorrow, and shock went on for several days, made more distressing by the fact that so few bodies were being recovered. The plane had fallen into a part of the ocean that was one hundred twenty feet deep, and the darkness of the depths made it difficult for divers to see. In what had to be a poignant experience for Judge, the FDNY divers arrived on the *Kevin C. Kane*, a fire department boat named after the young firefighter whose tragic death had convinced Judge to take on the chaplaincy.

Judge painfully and helplessly understood that among the families' deepest sorrows was their worry that they would not have the comfort of putting their loved ones' remains to rest. Two hundred thirty people had been on the flight, but by the fourth day, only 101 bodies had been found, with only forty-six of them identified. In an interview, Judge explained the depth of the horror the families were facing: "It's about death, shock, and separation, not knowing if the bodies will be found, not knowing if they'll be able to see them, to touch them. The medical examiner's report was quite graphic. People cried out loud. I found myself crying a number of times. I was feeling such pain with them. They told me stories about their daughter or son or husband or wife, and these people seemed so real to me that I couldn't believe they were dead. Someone's talking about a beautiful face that is now so broken, marred, and scarred."[24]

In addition to the one-on-one ministry, moving from one weeping and stunned person to the next, Judge also conducted communal ministry for the families. Giuliani had arranged for the priest to conduct an interfaith prayer service at a hangar at John F. Kennedy Airport, from where the plane had begun its fatal journey. Over two thousand grieving relatives and friends gathered in the immense space, many weeping inconsolably, as prayers in five languages from various traditions were offered.

The next day, Judge presided at another prayer service, this one on the beach at Smith's Point, Long Island, the closest land area to the spot in the ocean where the plane had crashed. The natural setting provided an opportunity for family members to erect miniature memorials with flowers, photos, and religious symbols. They prayed by the water's edge, as they offered flowers to the receding waves. Judge recognized the significance of this site: "The water's sacred to them."[25]

Every evening at the hotel, Judge offered Mass at an improvised altar, sparsely furnished for liturgy. People of all faiths, and some with no faith, attended. On one night he offered a reflection on how the people lost in the crash were being recovered in another way: "God is present, loving, smiling, having recovered our loved ones. They are in His presence illuminated by His smile, and warmed by His love. His kingdom is enriched this day, so enriched by so many beautiful souls. So much beauty. Our world is empty without them. Our hearts are broken, our sadness immense, our tears so abundant. We live our sorrow together."[26]

For at least two weeks more, Judge spent time at the hotel where victims' families gathered, often staying late into the night.

When Irish Eyes Are Smiling

In March of 1999, Judge began jotting in a journal, at the suggestion of a friend. On the inside front cover he described his various identities: "Some Mother's Son. 230 Dean St. [his boyhood address] Irish, Catholic, Democrat, priest, gay and more . . . No one (ever) asked me!"[27]

It is noteworthy that after identifying himself as having been born, the two top identities he mentions are his New York City origins and his ethnic heritage—both mentioned even before his faith. While a New Yorker through and through, Judge was also an Irishman at heart. On one of his trips to Ireland with the McDonalds, he fulfilled a lifelong dream: he received an official affirmation of Irish citizenship (something he had de facto by virtue of his parents having been born there). Judge's life in New York City was very much infused with his connection to the Emerald Isle.

Through his friendships with Steven McDonald and Brendan Fay, he was connected to diverse parts of the Irish community of New York. His heritage also provided instant common ground with many city officials, businessmen, and ecclesiastics. With such a large portion of the fire department being of Irish descent, Judge could not escape his ethnicity if he wanted to; he had a shamrock tattooed on one of his buttocks.[28]

His stature in the city's Irish community made him a natural choice to offer the benediction at the groundbreaking of New York's Irish Hunger Memorial. This monument was designed to commemorate the Irish potato famine of the mid-nineteenth century, which prompted a great migration to the United States through New York's harbor. It was the only public prayer he had ever written out beforehand, usually preferring to speak extemporaneously. Perhaps because of the strong connection he felt with the phenomenon the secular shrine commemorated, he wanted to be sure he got it right. The result was a hymn to Irish hardship, resilience, and faith:

> God, Father of our City, of our Nation, we stand here today a people well fed, warmly clothed and securely sheltered— We come to bless this spot where 150 years ago our ancestors came with only the strips of cloth on their backs, no house to sleep in and no potato—their staff of life—to fill their bellies. Nothing but faith, deep faith in you, faith in this blessed land you brought them to and faith in each

other. And so, with faith, they built the churches, they paved the streets and dug the subways. To them today we erect and dedicate this monument for all to see—their immigrant faith—and to renew our spirit of faith in you and each other on our immigrant journey to your heavenly kingdom. Amen.[29]

Among his many Irish friends and companions throughout the city was Malachy McCourt, the brother of Frank McCourt, author of *Angela's Ashes,* a popular memoir of Irish boyhood. Malachy was an author in his own right, as well as an actor and later a politician. McCourt was a mainstay in the New York Irish community, famous for his wide knowledge of Irish culture and lore, including writing a book about the beloved ballad, "Danny Boy." Judge, who loved to perform the Irish standards, was well known for his rendition of "Frankie and Johnny," including his signature gesture of taking out a handkerchief and pretending to cry when he got to the fatal ending.

Judge has often been compared to a bridge because of his unique ability to bring people together and his penchant for reconciling opposites. Because of his love of New York, he is often imagined as the Brooklyn Bridge, his favorite spot for contemplation. McCourt, however, offered an alternative image of Judge that expresses the priest's love for his native city: "There's a very old postcard of a giant Jesus looking in the window of the Empire State Building in those long, long robes," said McCourt. "And that was Mike Judge in New York. He was everywhere. Over the city. And ooohhh, how good it was to know he was there."[30]

CHAPTER SEVEN

9/11

Preparing for the Unknown Future

On May 11, 2001, Mychal Judge turned sixty-eight. Despite his still youthful and exuberant mind and spirit, his body had begun to feel its age, having experienced some serious illnesses, surgery, and a major complication because of a medicine mix-up. These did not bother him. He told friends he was planning on taking dance lessons, once he had become proficient in rollerblading.[1] He had recently written to a friend,

> I don't know what's next for me. I've had the best life of any friar in this house or of any priest I know. It's great to be a Franciscan. I take the ups and downs, the joys and sorrows, but that's life and I try to keep them balanced. I get down on my knees and pray, "Lord, help me." I have to get God in there because it's his world and he loves me and wants to hear from us. There are so many great things in my life. I have a wonderful, wonderful, wonderful, fruitful life—but I work at it and I pray continuously. I have to work at it because life is a mystery.[2]

A similar sense of the richness of his past and trust in the future pervaded a letter he wrote to friends and family in

February of 2001, as he had celebrated the fortieth anniversary of his priesthood. On that day, after presiding at two Masses at a Brooklyn parish, he made a personal and private pilgrimage to nearby St. Anselm's Parish, where his parents had been married. In the evening, he wrote:

> Someone asked me today if I had any idea, at all, what lay ahead of me on that [ordination] day. I knew I would say Mass and preach, that I would baptize, bury the dead, and perform weddings. The future was all in the hands of God. I could never have dreamt of all the parish years I would enjoy; the lively days in the dorm at Siena College, the extraordinary challenging year at Canterbury, England; the filling and emptying of the clothes closet for the homeless, the blessed ministry to the sick and dying with the AIDS virus; and now the joyful challenge as Chaplain of the New York City Fire Department. What a grace-filled Franciscan priesthood. . . . And the future? As on ordination day, only God knows, and he will reveal only what I need to know and to do each day. It will be wonderful—that's the way God is.[3]

At sixty-eight, he remembered the past lovingly but did not desire to dwell there, to relive glory days. He knew God yet had something for him to do. And like a true Franciscan, he trusted that whatever it was would be good.

Similar ideas clearly were on his mind on September 10, 2001, as he preached at a Mass celebrating the rededication of a newly renovated Bronx firehouse. In what would be his last sermon, he looked toward the future, whatever it would hold:

> We come to this house this morning to celebrate renewal, rejuvenation, new life. We come to thank God for the blessings for all the years that the good work has been done

here. . . . We can never thank God enough for the reality of the lives we have. So standing in his presence this morning—and truly this is a chapel—let us pause for a moment, perhaps close our eyes and thank God for some special blessing in our individual lives. You do what God has called you to do . . . you go out to do the job which is a mystery and a surprise . . . No matter how big the call, no matter how small, you have no idea what God's calling you to but he needs you. He needs me. He needs all of us. . . . Work together . . . and from this house, God's blessings go forth to this community. It's fantastic but very painful. We love the job. We all do. What a blessing that is—a difficult, difficult job, and God calls you to it and indeed he gives you a love for it so that a difficult job will be well done. Isn't he a wonderful guy? Isn't he good to you, to each one of you, and to me? Turn to him each day, put your faith and your trust and your hope and your life in his hands. And he'll take care of you. And you'll have a good life.[4]

Judge concluded the Mass by leading the congregation in singing "God Bless America."

Without knowing the tragedy that the next day held, Mychal Judge was ready for it.

September 11, 2001

Beyond the people who planned the September 11, 2001, attacks on the United States, few people could have imagined the ghastliness and devastation that would transpire that morning. The fact that this tragedy involved the ordinary events of taking a plane trip or going to a normal work day at the office made the destruction even more grisly, shocking, and terrifying. Having worked with firefighters for a decade, Mychal Judge knew only too well that every time the fire alarm rang, there was no way of knowing the unique complexities of danger that would be encountered. Yet even he would have been shocked by the immensity of the peril that so many would face that day.

Mychal joined the other men of his community for morning prayer at 8:00 a.m. on that crisp September morning. After eating a bowl of cold cereal, Judge went to his room for private prayer.

A few minutes before 9:00 a.m., there was an urgent knock on Judge's door. It was his confrere, Fr. Brian Carroll, OFM, who told him the horror he'd just witnessed. Just moments ago, walking along Manhattan's Sixth Avenue, just a block from the friary, he'd seen a large jetliner flying so low that he could read the numbers on the bottom of it. He watched this strange sight, a bit dumbfounded, following the plane's path as it headed downtown, until he saw it smash into the World Trade Center's North Tower.

"What? Oh my God. Oh my God," Judge said. He quickly changed from his brown Franciscan habit into black clerical garb. As he dressed, his beeper kept ringing with the alarm call. Carroll recalls that, somewhat typically and reflexively, Judge gave his head a spritz of hairspray before he left the room.[5] Another confrere, Fr. Fran Di Spigno, saw Judge leaving the friary with an uncharacteristically somber expression on his face. "Be well," he said to Di Spigno. "I'll see you later."[6]

In the few minutes that it took for Judge to rush across the street to the firehouse, the city was already experiencing a discordant chorus of shrill sirens blaring from all directions as rescue vehicles headed to the Twin Towers. Along with two off-duty firefighters, Judge jumped in his department car and raced downtown. It was a drive of about fifty blocks, or three miles. Upon arriving at the site, they were met by dozens of fire trucks responding to the scene. Judge put on his white fire department helmet and black uniform overcoat, stenciled with his name and the word *chaplain* on the back. In all, eventually over a thousand firefighters would respond, the largest job the department has ever faced.

The scene was already beyond the worst nightmare that even Dante could imagine in his description of the lowest rings of hell. At 9:03 a.m., a second plane had crashed into the South Tower. Faced with certain death from the flames already engulfing the buildings, occupants had begun to escape this torturous agony by jumping from windows from floors high up the 110-story buildings. Many fell for at least nine seconds before meeting their preferred death when their bodies crashed onto the pavement.

Judge's normal practice at fires and emergencies was to stand back from the site, allowing the firefighters to do their jobs. This time, he rushed into the building with them. One of the men from the 31st Street firehouse saw a look of sorrow on Judge's face that he had never seen before at even the worst blazes. Yet Mayor Giuliani, also on the scene, later recalled that as Judge moved past him to enter the building, Giuliani's request to "pray for us" was met with a characteristic twinkling smile, reminding the mayor, "I always do."[7] Fire Commissioner Thomas Von Essen was also nearby and recalled Judge's demeanor: "He looked really concerned. We didn't talk. We always talked. We always fooled around. But we didn't that morning."[8] Firefighter Christian Waugh saw Judge and remembered, "You could see it in his face. Usually, he's always saying hello to somebody. And this time he was just stone-faced."[9]

French documentary filmmakers who were in the North Tower caught some images of Judge as he stood by the building's windows as people dropped, one by one, to the plaza pavement below. Commenting on the footage of Judge in the film, Fr. Michael Duffy, OFM, has said, "If you look closely at that film, you'll see his lips moving. Now, for those of us who know him, he wasn't one that talked to himself. He was praying. And absolving people as they fell to their death."[10]

Although it was quickly apparent that they would never be able to contain a fire this enormous, firefighters flooded into the building to help the occupants escape to safety and to save anyone who may have been hurt. The awareness that they themselves would probably not emerge from the destroyed building did not deter them. "I love you like a brother. I may never see you again," one firefighter told his coworker as they rushed into the building. Another acknowledged, "We're going to be lucky if we survive this."[11]

Once inside the North Tower, Judge positioned himself with the fire department officers at the makeshift command center that had quickly been established in the building's lobby. Fire department commanders were trying to keep track of the endless stream of rescuers entering the tower, but the sheer number and the surrounding chaos made it a hopeless task. Judge was focused on the plaza where the jumpers were landing. A firefighter who survived recalled seeing Judge mumbling prayers, a troubled look on his face.

Fire department officials would soon learn about the other disasters that day: a plane crashed into the Pentagon, near Washington, DC, while another hijacked plane crashed into an empty field in rural Pennsylvania after being redirected by a group of passengers who thwarted the hijackers, saving countless other lives and preventing a national emergency of even greater scope.

The mayor and other city officials, wary of the intense danger in the North Tower, established another command center in a nearby building of the World Trade Center complex before eventually moving yet again to a firehouse about a half mile away from the disaster site. Giuliani and Von Essen moved to this location, and one of the firefighters encouraged Judge to move with them for his own safety. He stayed, explaining, "I'm not finished."[12]

Not even an hour had passed since he arrived on the scene when the French documentarians caught on film his expression of fear and horror as he stood frozen, but not ceasing to pray. His look of horror broke for just a brief second when firefighter Michael Angelini briefly greeted Judge. Angelini explained that his father and brother were also on scene rescuing people. "I'll say a prayer for your family," Judge assured him.[13]

Above the lobby was a mezzanine area that loomed over the spot where Judge had been standing and praying. The mezzanine was the location where most rescued occupants were fleeing the building. When a firefighter descended from the mezzanine and told Judge of the horrific devastation on that next landing, Judge's response was quick: "I'm needed up there. I have to go."

He climbed the stairs and continued his prayers there, attending to and anointing the wounded. A fire department photographer who was there recalled Judge's fervent prayer, spoken almost as a shout, "Jesus, please end this right now! God, please end this!"[14]

At 9:59 a.m., the loudest sound any of the rescuers had ever heard exploded in their ears. The South Tower was rapidly and totally crumbling into a heap. The immense destruction sent huge winds of smoke and debris into the North Tower lobby, billowing up to the mezzanine. Thick, black smoke temporarily blinded everyone present. As it cleared, rescuers stumbled around the darkness to check on one another.

Police Lieutenant William Cosgrove was staggering in the dark looking for an exit when he stumbled upon a body. Firefighter Angelini was nearby and saw a bit of white in the person's otherwise black collar. Deputy Fire Chief Peter

Hayden shined a flashlight on the victim's face and cried, "Oh my god, it's Father Mike."[15] Zachary Vause, a rookie firefighter who had been a paramedic, checked Judge's vitals and recognized the wheezing breaths as final ones. Vause's attempt at CPR proved futile. Judge's body had no pulse.

They thought he had been hit by a piece of falling debris, yet they could find no signs of traumatic injury, leaving the rescuers to assume that perhaps smoke inhalation or a heart attack triggered by the sheer fright of the moment had caused his death. With the need so great around them, they could have left his body where it lay. But the firefighters would not leave their chaplain's corpse abandoned. As they did with all of their comrades, they endeavored to remove the body from the scene.

Lieutenant Cosgrove and firefighter Vause enlisted the help of two men nearby, firefighter Waugh and Kevin Allen, an official of the city's office of emergency management, to remove his body from the scene. They carried him through the debris, down from the mezzanine in a dark and eerie silence punctuated only by the now-too-familiar grisly sound of jumpers hitting the pavement. One of the team found a broken plastic chair that must have been blown out of the building, and they placed his body on it. Down on the street level, daylight was beginning to return and the smoke was subsiding. John Maguire, a West Point graduate who was now a Goldman Sachs executive, was on the scene in his now-disheveled business attire, trying to be of help. He joined the quartet as they all began a somber procession through heaps of charred building parts, heading toward the nearest clear space on adjacent Vesey Street.[16]

As they plodded through the rubble with their precious burden, Reuters photographer Shannon Stapleton snapped a picture of this funereal procession of men covered in ash, fatigue and concern written on their faces, carrying the slumped body of Judge, clad in black shoes, black socks, black clerical garb, and his FDNY coat, lifeless limbs hanging over the sides of the chair, his head dropped to his right side.

Stapleton, a young photographer at the time, had been on a publicity shoot in Manhattan that morning when he received a call to get down to the World Trade Center. Arriving on the scene, he heard the eerily rhythmic sound of the floors of the South Tower collapsing upon each other. After scrambling around the disaster site, he noticed the five men carrying a body. Even in this unusual situation, he sensed that this was no routine mission. "The expression 'dead weight' is very true. And these were five big dudes that were really struggling to carry him in a chair," he remembers. "It wasn't like they were trying to save this guy. There was a reason why they were doing this."[17]

The photo quickly circled the globe in the first reporting on the devastation, and it remains one of the most iconic images of that day. It was called by some "a modern *Pietà*," referring to Michelangelo's haunting fifteenth-century statue of Mary holding the corpse of the dead Christ. Judge's twin sister, Dympna, later commented that the photo captured not only the priest's body but his spirit too: "It was such a portrait of his life. He was so close to the people he worked with."[18]

Out on the street, clear of the wreckage, the rescuers found an ambulance and placed Judge's body on a backboard. Police Officer Jose Alfonso Rodriguez directed them to nearby St. Peter's Church, New York's oldest Catholic parish, which had been slightly damaged by the debris. It had become a makeshift shelter for those seeking refuge from the sights, sounds, and smells of horror.

When the men who had carried his body asked at the church if a priest could administer last rites, a sacristan told them all the clergy were out attending to the panicked crowds in the streets. She assured them that in emergency situations any Catholic could administer these rites. So Rodriguez and Cosgrove offered both traditional and spontaneous prayers and blessings over Judge's body.[19] Very soon afterward, the area was enveloped once again by a deafening sound and suffocating, black smoke. The North Tower had collapsed.

After the effects of the second building's destruction had subsided, rescue workers carried Judge's body to a nearby office building that had been commandeered to act as a temporary morgue. When firefighters found Judge's body lying in a hallway, the sight of such an indecorous spot for their priest infuriated them, and they carried their beloved chaplain to what they considered a more appropriate, if only temporary, place of rest: back to St. Peter's Church, placing the body in front of the altar.

When word reached Fr. Peter Brophy, OFM, the pastor at St. Francis of Assisi Parish, that Judge had died, he sped to St. Peter's and asked the firefighters to bring the body back to West 31st Street. With no ambulances available, this simple request seemed impossible to fulfill, but the firefighters knew they had to act. Somehow, someone showed up with an FDNY ambulance and transported Judge's body back to the firehouse across from the friary. The ambulance was greeted by eighteen Franciscans in habit, who stood as an honor guard as the firemen carried Judge's body inside the firehouse, laid him on a bed, and placed a candle beside him. Together, the friars and firefighters prayed around the remains of the man whom both groups counted as a brother.

Before the friars could take him to a funeral home, they first had to take the body to Bellevue Hospital. City law dictated that victims of violent deaths must first be seen by a medical examiner before they are prepared for funeral rites. The hospital already had been receiving bodies of other victims, many of them firefighters and police officers, all awaiting identification and autopsy in order to be officially recorded.

Fr. Brophy insisted, however, that no autopsy be performed on Judge. When city officials insisted that the procedure must be done, one of the firefighters told them that the victim was Jewish and had to be buried before dusk.[20] Despite the fact that this explanation reflected neither Jewish burial custom nor, obviously, Judge's religious beliefs, the morgue official relented. He listed blunt force trauma to the head as the cause of death, though there was no evidence of this. The clerk typed out the first of the city's death certificates for the event, which was given the bureaucratic reference "DM," for "Disaster Manhattan." The number on the document was DM0001-01. Judge became known as 9/11's Victim Number 1.

Funeral

Three hundred forty-three firefighters died on 9/11, the largest number of firefighter deaths in a single incident in US history. (The second highest number, seventy-eight, occurred during a 1910 Montana wildfire that spread over three million acres.) The death toll from the four 9/11 attacks was 2,996 people, including the nineteen hijackers. In the days, weeks, and months that followed, the nation and the world mourned those who had died. The New York City metropolitan area, which had the largest number of victims, witnessed a seemingly unending procession of funerals. Because it would be weeks before rescuers would finish retrieving and attempting to identify human remains from the site, many of the victims' funerals were delayed.

Since Mychal Judge's body was removed from the site prior to the North Tower's collapse and because his remains were totally intact, he had been readily identified, and his funeral became one of the first in New York City. Because of his renown among the firefighters, city officials, and people of all walks of life, it was also one of the largest and most public of the 9/11 funerals.

The funeral Mass was held at St. Francis of Assisi Parish, where he had first encountered the Franciscans as a young boy, where he had ministered for the last decade of his life, and which was across the street from the firehouse he used as his home base for chaplaincy work. The date was September 15, the twenty-third anniversary of his sobriety. Over three thousand people attended the Mass, presided over by New York's Cardinal Edward Egan. So many mourners showed up that the city had to close off the street and set up jumbotrons outside the church for those who could not be accommodated inside.

Among the many politicians in the church were former President Bill Clinton and former First Lady Hillary Clinton, along with their daughter, Chelsea. The president lamented that Judge's death was a "special loss," commenting to the press that "we should lift his life up as an example of what has to prevail. We have to be more like Father Mike than [like] the people who killed him."[21] Mrs. Clinton spoke at the Mass, describing Judge as a "bearer of light" who gave those he met "gifts of laughter and love."[22] She would later recall their breakfast together in Washington, DC: "He lit up the White House as he lit up every place he ever found himself."[23]

Brian Carroll, who had been a friar at the time, recalls walking around the crowd of overflow mourners outside the church, witnessing the diversity of common people whose lives had been touched by Judge. Among them, he noticed someone he knew as a street person who was living with AIDS. Carroll didn't immediately recognize the man because he was dressed so differently than usual: he was wearing a tuxedo that he purchased at a thrift shop because he wanted to honor Judge's memory by dressing properly.

"The whole scene was very Franciscan, very Mychal," Carroll recalled. "There was the nobility of society mixed in with the poor and humble people. It showed the depth and breadth of those Mychal reached out to."[24]

As Judge had requested in funeral details he had provided his community in preparation for eventual death, Fr. Michael Duffy, OFM, his friend from his pastoral ministry days in New Jersey, offered the homily. Duffy told many stories from his life with Judge and described him as "truly, purely Franciscan, simple, joyful, life loving and laughter." He highlighted Judge's simplicity by describing a recurrent encounter he often had with him:

> He would say to me once in a while, "Michael Duffy"—he always called me by my full name—"Michael Duffy, you know what I need?"
>
> "No, what Mike?"
>
> "Absolutely nothing. I don't need a thing in the world. I am the happiest man on the face of the earth." And then he would go on for ten minutes, telling me how blessed he felt. "I have beautiful sisters. I have nieces and nephews. I have my health. I'm a Franciscan priest. I love my work. I love my ministry." And he would go on, and always conclude by looking up to heaven and saying, "Why am I so blessed? I don't deserve it. Why am I so blessed?" But that's how he felt all his life.

Duffy also mused about the spiritual significance of Judge dying while he ministered during this catastrophe of immense proportions:

> Mychal Judge could not have ministered to them all. It was physically impossible in this life but not in the next. And I think that if he were given his choice, he would prefer to have happened what actually happened. He passed through the other side of life, and now he can continue doing what he wanted to do with all his heart. And the next few weeks, we're going to have names added, name after name of people, who are being brought out of that rubble. And Mychal Judge is going to be on the other side of death to greet them instead of sending them there. And he's going to greet them with that big Irish smile. He's going to take them by the arm and the hand and say, "Welcome, I want to take you to my Father." And so, he can continue doing in death what he couldn't do in life.

Duffy concluded by reminding the congregation about a central tenet of the Christian view of death: the flesh may no longer be alive, but the spirit continues: "And so, this morning we come to bury Mike Judge's body but not his spirit. We come to bury his mind but not his dreams. We come to bury his voice but not his message. We come to bury his hands but not his good works. We come to bury his heart but not his love. Never his love."[25]

CHAPTER EIGHT

"I Am Alive as I Can Be"

The story of the tragic death of Fr. Mychal Judge, who previously had been known primarily within the New York metropolitan area, made him known around the planet. As the most prominent religious figure who died in the 9/11 attacks, he became a symbol for the selflessness, courage, heroism, and faith lived out during a moment of great fear, sorrow, and despair. For many, Judge emerged as the patron saint of this catastrophe, mirroring goodness when evil was so apparent.

The interest of journalists and others was sparked by his story, which seemed to be a bright light of hope during this time of dark disaster. As his renown grew, more and more people stepped forward with stories of how he touched their lives. The world began to get a clearer view of this friar whose life journey and ministry revealed a concern for outcasts, a willingness to takes risks in his ministry, and a complexity of personality underneath his monochrome clerical garments.

Was Mychal Judge Gay?

One facet of Judge's life that received scrutiny after his death has been his sexual orientation. On September 18, 2001, exactly one week after 9/11, a journalist revealed a detail about Mychal Judge that added to the public's interest in this remarkable man. In a *Village Voice* article that offered short descriptions of some of the 9/11 victims, the section on Judge contained the following paragraph:

> To friends, he was known as a gay man who appreciated the *Gay USA* show and celebrated the city's "gorgeous men" by saying, "Isn't God wonderful?" When his close friend, gay activist Brendan Fay, started a St. Patrick's parade in Queens last year that included gay groups, Judge helped him fund it and showed up in his brown friar's robe to put the church on the side of the oppressed, even as Catholic officialdom was urging a boycott. He frequently donated clothes to the Out of the Closet Thrift Shop for gay and AIDS causes on East 81st Street. He was a longtime member of Dignity, the gay Catholic group. In recent years, he came out to many of those he loved, including Fire Commissioner Tom Von Essen, who warmly accepted him.[1]

This story was followed a few weeks later by an October 9 *Village Voice* article[2] that reported on a 9/11 remembrance service held at New York's Gay and Lesbian Center on October 1 where Judge was honored with energetic applause. Testimonies began to emerge from people who said that Judge identified as gay privately, but not publicly. Along with the acknowledgment of his orientation came stories of his ministry to the LGBT community, which had previously not been well known. Those stories attested to the same generous, affirming, selfless care that Judge exhibited with his former parishioners, the firefighters, and in his other public ministries.

Some of those with whom Judge ministered were surprised but not offended to learn this news about their beloved priest. Lieutenant David Fullam, who was stationed in the firehouse just across the street from Judge's friary, said they were aware of the priest's inclusive ministry: "We knew that he ministered to the AIDS population and the gay population." Fullam added that some firefighters were very surprised when they learned after Judge's death that he was gay, but they still accepted him. "We didn't care if he was gay or straight. We loved him."[3] The reaction of another firefighter who was known among acquaintances for making anti-gay remarks was only slightly different. When he heard about Judge's orientation after 9/11, his reaction was, "If somebody really convinced me of that, all you could do was tell me I had my first gay friend."[4]

Thomas Von Essen, who served as fire commissioner while Judge was a chaplain, was one firefighter who was not surprised. In a 2017 interview with the *Irish Post*, Von Essen said that he was aware of Judge's sexuality even before he assumed the department's top office: "I actually knew about his homosexuality when I was in the Uniformed Firefighters Association. I kept the secret, but then he told me when I became commissioner five years ago. He and I often laughed about it, because we knew how difficult it would have been for the other firemen to accept it as easily as I had. I just thought he was a phenomenal, warm, sincere man, and the fact that he was gay just had nothing to do with anything."[5]

Yet not everybody was happy with, or even believed, this news about Judge's sexual identity. Some people alleged that LGBT advocates were using Judge's public status as a moral hero to push for greater acceptance of homosexuality. Still others believed that since Judge was not only a priest but an exemplary one, there was no way that he could possibly also be gay; they thought the two identities totally incompatible. They did not want a religious hero's reputation to be tainted by identifying him with a stigmatized identity.

In a 2002 interview with *The New York Times*, city official Brian Mulheren, a friend of Judge's, said, "To say he was gay after he was dead, and to say he said it, that's something I can't understand. There are a lot of people out there who are opportunists. We knew who he was. He was one of the finest human beings on the earth."[6]

Catholic lawyer Dennis Lynch penned an online article that became widely quoted in which he argued that advocates were claiming Judge was gay to promote their own agendas. His evidence was that although he himself was close to Judge, the priest never disclosed a gay orientation to him. "Concerned that Father Mike was being used by homosexual activists, I began to contact many people who knew Father Mike for as long as I knew him or longer," he wrote. "I wanted the truth about Father Mike to be published. Not one of these longtime friends ever heard or saw anything that Father Mike did to indicate he was homosexual. I personally spent weeks at a time with Father Mike where he and I spoke about many personal matters. Not once was there even a suggestion that Father Mike was 'gay.' Father Mike was a celibate Catholic Priest and nothing more."[7]

What Does It Mean to Be Gay?

The presumptions about gay and lesbian people exhibited in Mulheren's and Lynch's reactions need to be examined, because these attitudes shed light on why Judge would have been circumspect about revealing his orientation publicly while alive. Such an examination is important because such presumptions, in both the general society and the church, continue to cause discrimination against LGBTQ people.

One strong presumption is that gay people are de facto in opposition to faith institutions, uninterested in living lives of faith within a community of faith, and thus cannot be holy people. According to this thinking, the overwhelming public evidence of Judge's goodness and holiness disproved that he was gay. How could someone whom many were unofficially proclaiming to be a saint also have been part of a community that many people thought of as degenerate? Empirical evidence shows, however, that many gay and lesbian people have strong connections to faith communities and lead deeply spiritual lives.

Another presumption is that all gay and lesbian people are sexually active—and usually deviously and promiscuously so. Cultural stereotypes paint gay men, in particular, as oversexed and predatory. In this line of thinking, identifying as gay means admitting that one is sexually active. Yet many people come to awareness of a gay or lesbian sexual orientation without engaging in sexual activity. Instead, they recognize their orientation by acknowledging the permanency and strength of same-gender attractions, emotions, and fantasies without, or before, engaging in any sexual activity.

These misunderstandings led some to assume that if Judge identified as gay, then it meant that he was admitting he had not honored his vow of celibacy and perhaps, even further, that he was promiscuous. They would have suspected him of leading a double life. No evidence exists to show that either of these possibilities was the case. Although in some popular understandings, homosexuality is about desire for carnal pleasure, the more accurate insight is that homosexuality is about the gender of the person with whom one falls in love. A number of people who publicly declare that they are gay or lesbian never choose to engage in sexual activity. They become personally and emotionally fulfilled with strong interpersonal relationships.

Judge did not fit these stereotypes, which led many to assume that he was heterosexual. Instead of the reigning falsehood that gay men are effeminate, Judge was quite "masculine." Instead of the cinematic image of gay men as physically slight with delicate features, Judge was a tall, strapping man, with a rugged appearance. Instead of the presumption that gay men were cowardly, Judge showed great courage by involving himself with the dangerous profession of firefighting. Instead of wearing colorful, outrageous, flamboyant clothing, Judge routinely wore his brown Franciscan habit or his fire department uniform.

As gay men have become more visible in society in recent years, many of these stereotypes, thankfully, have evaporated. Gay men are now known to be war heroes, professional athletes, government leaders, corporate businessmen—and holy priests and church ministers. One person whose actions helped to dispel that image was Mark Bingham, the gay man on United Airlines Flight 93 on September 11, 2001, who organized the passengers to resist the hijackers, forcing the plane to crash in a Pennsylvania farm field instead of causing many more deaths and unimaginable destruction by reaching its intended target, the White House.

Exacerbating people's cognitive dissonance about Judge's identity was that immediately following his death there was scant evidence to show he was gay. Only personal testimony from a select number of his wide and varied friends supported this fact. This paucity of evidence is understandable given the cultural, social, and ecclesial milieus in which Judge grew up and lived. The open visibility and acceptance of LGBTQ people today makes it easy to forget that in the past people were not as open about their identities. The default was to conceal, not disclose. Even when a nascent discussion of the issues began to arise in the 1970s and 1980s, old habits designed for self-protection lived on. For someone like Judge, who came of age in the 1940s and 1950s, concealment felt natural.

Concealment was an even stronger strategy for gay and lesbian people in religious professions. While same-sex attraction was not spoken of frequently in church circles during Judge's formative years, when it was mentioned, it was almost always in the most condemnatory language and tones. This attitude would have been especially prevalent in seminaries and religious formation programs, likely due to the fact that they were same-sex environments. What Judge knew about how people perceived homosexuality made him recognize that not everyone would be able to accept this information in a way that would allow him to continue as an effective minister.

It makes sense that Judge would have shared this personal information primarily with others in the LGBT community where he knew it would be understood free of unfounded fears and stereotypes. As someone concerned about others' feelings, he also knew that they would not be offended by such information. Many of the gay and lesbian people Judge knew said that they knew he was gay even without a direct statement from him. To understand how this assumption could be justified requires understanding the coded way that gay and lesbian people often spoke with one another at the time.

Because an outright revelation could put a gay or lesbian person at risk of losing family, friends, employment, and housing, a common practice among many in this community was to use less direct ways of communicating with others assumed to be gay or lesbian. Salvatore Sapienza, who worked with Judge's HIV/AIDS ministry team, recalled that while none of the members of that group ever made a statement revealing a gay identity, those who were gay used a coded form of communication, an insider language, to let themselves be known to one another.

"We would laugh and joke in a particular way," Sapienza remembered. They used words and expressions that were part of the gay community idiom. Judge frequently communicated this way. If they were walking together in the street and noticed some attractive men, Judge would jovially say, "Thank God for such beauty." The comments were always positive, never vulgar or graphic, but were clearly designed to subtly reveal himself. While ministering with HIV/AIDS patients, almost all of whom were gay men, Judge did not discuss his sexual identity. But Sapienza observed that with a glance, a joke, a smile, or a wink, Judge would let the gay men know that he personally understood the stigma they faced because of their sexual identity.[8]

The Diary

Instead of dying down, the issue of Judge's sexuality continued to arise periodically. In 2002, the Catholic publishing house Paulist Press published *Father Mychal Judge: An Authentic American Hero*. In this first complete biography, Catholic journalist Michael Ford researched the issue of Judge's sexuality as part of his study of the priest's life. He demonstrated that Judge's journey with his sexuality was integral to his development as a person and as a priest. Ford's account offered the first complete set of facts and testimonies that pushed the discussion away from rumors and rebuttals.[9]

In 2006, Equality Forum, a national LGBTQ organization, produced a documentary about Judge entitled *Saint of 9/11*. In the film, several Catholic ministers discuss Judge's gay identity, noting that it made him more effective in reaching out to people pastorally. The film did not focus on his sexuality but viewed it as an important influence on the positive way he connected with others.[10]

In 2008, more concrete evidence came to light. In 1999, two years before Judge's death, a gay friend had encouraged Judge to keep a journal in which he could write about his sexual identity openly. The journal was a short-lived exercise, extending only a few months and extending through fifty-seven pages. Friends said Judge never had time to write because of his busy schedule. Judge's twin sister, Dympna, gave journalist Michael Daly access to the journal, and he included some excerpts in his 2008 biography of Judge.

As noted previously, Judge began the diary with some self-identification on the inside front cover: "Some Mother's Son. 230 Dean St. [his boyhood address] Irish, Catholic, Democrat, priest, gay and more . . . No one (ever) asked me!"[11]

The entries that followed chronicle his struggle with being private about his sexuality. Part of this struggle was due to the fact that he genuinely accepted the gift of sexuality and his own sexuality in particular. He wanted the freedom to share that reality with others: "I thought of my gay self and how the people I meet never get to know me fully—and why? Because it is not acceptable. No one, absolutely no one lives two fuller separate lives as I do. Little wonder I am so tired at day's end."[12]

Judge had learned to appreciate his sexual feelings and was grateful to God for them, even though he was aware that the church often sent disapproving messages about sexual attractions:

A thousand thoughts and desires run through my mind at everybody I see. But only for a moment—Drives, desires, passions, energy, excitement, yearning and all the rest. I see the beauty, how God created it and how, in a sense, the Church scorns your dwelling on it—Sexual, sinful—Hand in hand—But they are not connected at all. I love, I applaud the beauty of God's handiwork. . . . Sexually, I am alive as I can be. The thoughts, the drives, the desire are there always. Can't see enough on the street . . . and I am grateful for it . . . And you, Lord, are always there and you so nicely remind me to call on you and show me your presence. I love you. . . .

Well, here I am . . . I'm somehow started, I think, on this new journey—not sure where it is taking me, how I am to go, etc. etc. But I keep praying and asking for guidance and leadership. It is a real test of my faith and belief and that God is there.[13]

These and other passages in the Judge diary reveal that, despite the struggles, he had come to a healthy and holy acceptance of his sexuality and its place in his life as a committed Franciscan friar. Like any partial record, these brief writings make some readers wish for fuller explanations. How did he come to such an acceptance of his identity? If his experience were typical, this process would have included many moments of confusion, guilt, shame, despair, constraint, and even doubts about a loving God. But it also would have included many powerful moments of clarity, affirmation, joy, courage, liberation, and faith in a God of love who made human creatures with the capacity for love. From the bits of information that he left about his self-acceptance and communing with God, these latter moments were surely in abundance.

His Close Friend

One important part of the story of Judge's sexuality has to do with his relationship with an openly gay man named Al Alvarado. During the last ten years of his life, Judge spent a large amount of his time with Alvarado, a New York City nurse. According to Alvarado, their bond with one another was very strong, and evidence from Judge's hand indicates the same. Soon after meeting him, Judge wrote in his calendar: "ALA Intense Committed." "ALA" was his shorthand for "Al Alvarado," and it appeared frequently in his calendar as an appointment.[14]

Judge's friend Brian Carroll reported that Alvarado was very special in Judge's life and that he loved the nurse very much. Judge believed that God put special people in his life, and he considered Alvarado one of them, Carroll said. "Al was someone with whom he could have tender conversations, someone who was there to take care of him the way that he cared for so many other people," Carroll explained. The relationship nourished Judge, and Alvarado was his "brother, best friend, confidante, someone very close to his heart." Judge was always giving to others, Carroll observed, so it was important to him to have a relationship in which he was able to receive too.[15]

Biographer Daly, who interviewed Alvarado, confirmed that Alvarado had a special place in Judge's life but was convinced that their relationship did not lead to Judge breaking his vow of celibacy. Alvarado knew that Judge's priestly commitment was primary in his life. He told Daly, "[Judge] told me going into it. He told me at the beginning he could only see me so much: it could only go so far. . . . My rival was God," Alvarado told Daly.[16] Daly concluded,

"Judge had long ago declared himself a servant to his God, a groom only to Christ."[17]

While eyebrows were raised about Judge's intense relationship with Alvarado, it is important to remember the Franciscan also had intense emotional and time-heavy relationships with some fire department widows. For years after firefighter John Drennan's death, Judge called his widow, Vina, almost every night, but no question of any kind of impropriety has been suggested. The double standard reflects the presumptions mentioned earlier that gay men are hyper-sexual and that gay priests must be living double lives. Like everyone else, celibate people still have emotional needs, desires for interpersonal intimacy, and the ability to give and receive love, which their vow does not erase or deny, and they can fulfill these feelings through close relationships and commitments.

Alvarado was unable to attend Judge's funeral, because the church was already filled and there was no room for him when he arrived. He watched the funeral on one of the screens set up on the street with the overflow crowd. Fr. Christopher Keenan, OFM, recognized him and stood with him as Judge's coffin was carried out of church. Brian Carroll, then a friar, greeted Alvarado and arranged for him to ride in the bus the friars were using to go to the cemetery.

Why Does Judge's Sexuality Matter?

In March 2011, almost ten years after 9/11, a former classmate of Judge's, who had left the community as a young man and later married, told a reporter that Judge had shared his gay identity with him. Dr. J. Rene Wilett, a clinical psychologist, recalled that Judge had the ability to acknowledge personal problems and deal with them honestly. During a conversation when they were in their forties, Judge casually and matter-of-factly told Willett that he was gay. "In one sense it didn't matter," Wilett commented, "and in another sense it was critically important, because he was a recovering alcoholic, a gay man, and a holy priest, and those were all bridges he used to reach the people."[18]

Wilett's comment illuminates an important tension: Judge's sexuality is, at the same time, one of the most and least important things about him. A homosexual orientation in itself does not diminish a person's human abilities or a capacity for relationship with God. The cultural and ecclesial disapproval of it, however, means that a person's life can be significantly shaped, positively or negatively, by these forces. In Judge's case, the experience appears to have been overwhelmingly positive.

Still, his sexual identity was only one of many influences on his spirituality and ministry. His traditional Irish Catholicism and his love of New York City provided him with strong faith and a natural predisposition to the diversity of humanity. His Franciscan formation and community gave him an understanding of God's immanence in the world and God's intense love for all created beings. The 12-Step principles and fellowship he treasured allowed him to accept his brokenness and to humbly realize his limitations. His time with the firefighters offered him a living example of courage and self-sacrificing risk.

Having a stigmatized sexual orientation surely helped Judge reach out to those whom society wanted to pretend weren't there. The marginalization and repression Judge experienced most likely contributed to his sympathetic approach to people as they experienced confusing and troublesome situations. The courage it took to accept his identity prepared him for the courage he would need to minister in extremely dangerous emergencies.

Understanding the spiritual gifts that Mychal Judge's sexuality inspired are important not just for comprehending his life, but because it contributes to the ongoing discussion about LGBTQ issues in the Catholic Church, particularly with regard to priesthood. Recent Vatican documents have suggested that gay men cannot be effective priests and should not be ordained. In 2005, the Vatican's Congregation for Catholic Education issued an "Instruction Concerning the Criteria for the Discernment of Vocations with Regard to Persons with Homosexual Tendencies in View of Their Admission to the Seminary and to Holy Orders." Published with the explicit approval of Pope Benedict XVI, the brief document said that a candidate for the priesthood must have achieved "affective maturity" in order to be able "to relate correctly to both men and women" so that he could develop "a true sense of spiritual fatherhood towards the Church community that will be entrusted to him." Because of this and because "deep-seated homosexual tendencies" are "objectively disordered," the document said, the church cannot admit gay men to the seminary or ordain them: "One must in no way overlook the negative consequences that can derive from the ordination of persons with deep-seated homosexual tendencies."[19] This approach to gay candidates was reaffirmed over a decade later, in a 2016 document by the Congregation for the Clergy intended to update the church's formal guidelines (or *ratio fundamentalis*) for the formation of priests. Entitled "The Gift of the Priestly Vocation," the document quoted several key sentences from the 2005 document.[20]

Pope Francis famously demonstrated a sort of nonjudgmental openness to the idea of a priest being gay, when he responded in 2013 to a question about the presence of gay men in the priesthood with the question, "Who am I to judge?" And yet in 2018, he reiterated the warning about "affective maturity" in an answer he offered to an interview question about gay men in the priesthood. He stated that a priest's homosexuality is "a very serious matter, which must be discerned adequately from the beginning with the candidates," and emphasized that the church "must be demanding" because homosexuality is "fashionable" in society "and this mentality, in some way, also affects the life of the Church."[21]

Yet, despite these stringent prohibitions and attitudes, the church indeed does have a significant number of gay men in the priesthood, episcopacy, and religious life (as well as lesbian sisters and LGBTQ lay ministers and employees). Unfortunately, they often serve the church under a shadow of fear and shame. The ecclesial closet means that church leaders who develop policy never fully understand how many gifts LGBTQ people bring to the church and how much the church's life depends on them. Church members never get to see the holiness of LGBTQ lives. LGBTQ people, particularly youth, have no role models of integrating their sexual identity with their love for God.

Judge had hoped that the example of his life would help people become more accepting of gay people. In one entry to the journal that he hoped would be a testament about his sexual identity, he wrote that he hoped his known goodness might persuade people to be less homophobic when they found out he was gay: "Every group can have an advocate—good, bad, or indifferent. Maybe, maybe a book in a chapter by Mychal Judge—well respected, loved by many, faithful to his profession, loyal to his community and friends, compassionate beyond bounds—you would like to be in his company, to be his friend—well if he is gay there must be something okay with 'them'—you could talk so freely, explain so much, release fears, explain the pain, show the joy and give peace to so many."[22]

The life of Fr. Mychal Judge, OFM, provides a roadmap of how, through patient listening, humble acceptance, courageous vulnerability, and welcoming any and all people, the church can take steps to improve its relationship with its LGBTQ people and all on the margins.

Posthumous Honors

Fr. Mychal Judge's memory has been honored across the United States and elsewhere. His legacy as a gregarious servant and empathetic priest has invited many diverse tributes accorded to his memory and the causes for which he advocated.

The portion of West 31st Street between Sixth and Seventh Avenues in Manhattan, where St. Francis of Assisi Church and the firehouse from which Judge worked, was renamed Fr. Mychal F. Judge Street. New York City also christened one of its waterway ferries the *Father Mychal Judge*. This ferry was used to rescue passengers from US Airways Flight 1549 when it made a safe emergency landing in the Hudson River in 2009.

The United States Congress passed The Mychal Judge Police and Fire Chaplains Public Safety Officers Benefit Act, which guarantees federal death benefits to any public safety officer who dies in the line of duty. Passed in 2002, the benefits were retroactive to September 11, 2001. The act also extended death benefits to any person the officer designates, including same-gender domestic partners, the first time the federal government had ever provided for members of such unions.

Judge's fire helmet was presented to Pope John Paul II at the Vatican.

In the Irish village of Keshcarrigan, from which Judge's father emigrated, the Father Mychal Judge Memorial was built, and a ceremony is held there annually on September 11. The land for the memorial belonged to Judge's ancestors.

The nation of France named Judge into the National Order of the Legion of Honor, its highest award for military and civil accomplishments.

In September 2002, Judge's friend Steven McDonald organized the Fr. Mychal Judge Walk of Remembrance, an annual event to commemorate those who died in the 9/11 attacks. The walk begins at St. Francis of Assisi Parish, and it follows the route that Judge took to the World Trade Center on 9/11, stopping at firehouses and police precincts along the way, and ending at St. Peter's Church, which had been Judge's temporary resting place after his body was rescued.

The Franciscan Friars established a relief fund for homeless people in Judge's memory. St. Anthony Shrine, the Franciscan urban ministry center in Boston that had been Judge's first priestly assignment, established the Father Mychal Judge Recovery Center to provide counseling and treatment referrals to those struggling with addictions.

Siena College in Albany, New York, where Judge ministered, posthumously awarded him the degree of Doctor of Humane Letters. The Gay and Lesbian Alumni of the University of Notre Dame and St. Mary's College posthumously awarded Judge their Thomas Dooley Award, in recognition to his ministry to the LGBT community. St. Bonaventure University in Olean, New York, Judge's alma mater, established the Father Mychal Judge Center for Irish Exchange and Understanding to study globalization issues in the context of Ireland.

The Brooklyn Diocese instituted the Fr. Mychal Judge Memorial Award, presented at its Great Irish Fair fundraiser.

Alvernia University, a Franciscan school in Reading, Pennsylvania, named a new residence hall after Judge.

The New York Press Club established The Rev. Mychal Judge Heart of New York Award, an annual honor presented "for the story or series that is most complimentary of New York City. Good news about people, places, and deeds."[23]

In 2011, on the tenth anniversary of the 9/11 tragedies, All Saints Parish in Syracuse, New York, unveiled a statue of first responders carrying Judge's body. Part of the reason for erecting the statue was to affirm LGBTQ Catholics, to whom the parish offers a special welcome.[24]

In 2015, a statue of Judge was erected in St. Joseph's Park in East Rutherford, New Jersey, across the street from the parish of the same name where he ministered for many years. In the city's 9/11 Memorial Park, his name is on a plaque along with other residents who died in the September 11 attacks.

Chicago's Legacy Walk, an outdoor museum of forty bronze plaques honoring notable LGBTQ people, includes one for Fr. Mychal Judge. In 2017, he was inducted into the Irish American Hall of Fame, also in Chicago.

The Irish-American Celtic rock band Black 47 composed and recorded the song "Mychal" on their album *New York Town*.

John Tranchitella performs the one-man play *My Will and My Life*, written by Fr. Harry Cronin, CSC, and directed by Christopher P. Kelly. The play tells the story of Mychal Judge from the perspective of a character who experienced the ministry of Fr. Mychal at an AA meeting.

And, of course, he is listed at the National 9/11 Memorial on the complex of the new World Center, near the South

Pool, on Panel S-18, along with the other first responders who died.

Sainthood

Since his death, there has been some progress toward having Judge canonized as a Catholic saint, a status that many believers already informally accord him. In July 2017, Pope Francis provided a new possible pathway for his sainthood with the *motu propio Maiorem hac dilectionem*. The document formally established the criteria of "a free and voluntary offer of life and heroic acceptance *propter caritatem* [that is, out of love] of a certain and untimely death" as cause for canonization.[25]

Immediately following this change, Fr. Luis Fernando Escalante, a postulator for the Vatican's Congregation for Saints, opened an inquiry into the life and death of Mychal Judge by interviewing people who knew him personally.[26] But the Order of Friars Minor, Judge's Franciscan community, was opposed to seeking the priest's canonization, and their support would have helped the progress of the canonization process. In 2002, when calls for Judge's canonization had already begun, Fr. John Felice, OFM, then the provincial of his community, told *The New York Times* that such a status would define Judge too narrowly and would even be an injustice to him: "A lot of what Mychal was about was admirable. I'm just a little leery of putting it into a context that shoves a person away from our human experience, and makes them less effective as models for everyday living. It's better to keep the real Mychal alive and well in your brain. I think he has a lot more to say than a Mychal with a halo over his head."[27]

In September 2021, just a week before the twentieth anniversary of 9/11, Fr. Kevin Mullen, OFM, at that time the community's provincial, answered an *Associated Press* reporter's question about whether the Franciscans would work for the priest's canonization by saying, "We are very proud of our brother's legacy and we have shared his story with many people. We leave it to our brothers in the generations to come to inquire about sainthood."[28]

As this book was going to print, a grassroots movement has been developing to form an association that would sponsor the research and administrative work needed to promote Fr. Judge's canonization cause. As the one universally recognized casualty of 9/11, his sainthood would be a symbol for all the victims and their families, but also for so many of the groups, mainstream and marginal, with whom he ministered. If such a group is organized, it would take on the work of raising funds and directing the necessary research needed for the canonization process.

His grave in Holy Sepulchre Cemetery in Totowa, New Jersey, has become a place of pilgrimage, visited by people from all over the world, some who knew him and some who didn't. Firefighters, LGBTQ people, New Jersey parishioners, recovery fellowship members, Franciscans, and many others leave flowers, small figurines, and other symbolic gifts to remind themselves and others of the friar who preached the unconditional love of God to all.

When the World Seems Its Darkest

Father Mychal Judge ran into the fiery inferno of a crumbling building as others were running out of it. Why did he put himself into a dangerous situation when the option to stay in a safety zone was available to him? While we can't learn the motivation from him directly, the story of his life provides enough evidence to construct a plausible answer.

By running into the North Tower of the World Trade Center so that he could minister to those suffering, Judge was responding in a way that had become second nature to him. His sixty-eight years of life, prayer, community, and ministry had made him into a person who valued relationship over self, service over prestige, the suffering Christ over power and riches.

Judge's decision to act on 9/11 was not because he was a superhero. He would be the first to admit so. He had no special powers that were unique to him. He would say just the opposite. Whatever power he had was a power that is available to all. Judge's spiritual strength came from his utter dependence upon God to care for him and guide him. No doubt his childhood Irish Catholicism began teaching him this habit, but certainly his Franciscan formation developed it, and his AA spirituality confirmed it in him. In his 1999 journal, he prayed, "Oh Lord—you know me so well—I can't hide from you—I have nothing, nothing to fear—All I have to do is your will and all will be well—Make it known to me."[1]

The prayer that he composed for himself and frequently shared with others reflects this attitude (as well as his gift for self-deprecation): "Lord, take me where you want me to go. Let me meet who you want me to meet. Tell me what you want me to say, and keep me out of your way."

Throughout his lifetime, Judge had developed a particularly personal and intimate relationship with God. His ministry flowed from this relationship. His experience of God's goodness and grace inspired him to want to share these gifts with other people, to help them experience that too. His habit of spontaneously blessing people and breaking into conversational prayer during his ordinary encounters with others was a sign of this intimacy that he experienced with God.

As a true Franciscan, he didn't need to look to the heavens for God. He found God in the world. He had developed the ability to see God's presence in the most unlikely of places. God for him was a part of everything, and everything in the world could teach people something about God. He didn't exhort people to be good; he encouraged them to see the goodness that God had already placed in their lives. If people could not see that, he was always ready to point out their goodness for them. He reached out to people regardless of whether or not they responded to his gentle invitation to recognize God in their lives.

Judge was no Pollyanna, though. His own experiences of brokenness were enough reminders to prevent him from pretending that pain and suffering did not exist. Yet his life had also taught him that pain and suffering were not the end of the story. His heart could be so available to other people's pain because he was keenly aware of what pain felt like. He could reach out to the alienated because he knew the experience of marginalization. He had a gift for accepting people as they were because he had come to accept himself. He could build community so naturally because community and companionship were experiences that he sought for himself too.

Judge's life touched on so many of the most important social and cultural issues of the closing half of the twentieth century and the brink of the twenty-first. He grew up in the immigrant church, embraced commitment in a world of instantaneous change, ministered in the wake of the great changes of Vatican II, confronted addiction in an "anything goes" culture, resolved questions of sexuality in an era of permissiveness, attended to the needs of the poor and marginalized during a time of immense prosperity, cared for people with the most dreaded, deadly, and debilitating disease of his era, and faced the horror of international terrorism.

Most importantly, Judge's life story asks and answers one of the most important questions of the twenty-first-century environment: In a world where unspeakable tragedies occur with breathtaking frequency and where so many traditional patterns of civilized human relationships keep breaking down, where does one find God? Put another way, where was God on 9/11?

Judge would encourage us to see that God was not absent on that day. God was present in the heroic acts of self-sacrifice that the first responders offered. God was present in the many quiet acts of care and concern people offered to injured and frightened people, and to those who were mourning inconsolably. And God was present in the prayerful witness of Fr. Mychal Judge, who could have stayed on the sidelines but who knew that his place was to be with the people he loved and served. Judge's life reminds us that we are responsible for manifesting God's presence in the world, especially when the world seems its darkest.

Notes

Chapter 1—pages 1–16

1. Michael Daly, *The Book of Mychal: The Surprising Life and Heroic Death of Father Mychal Judge* (New York: St. Martin's Press, 2008), 11.

2. Daly, *Book of Mychal*, 5.

3. Daly, 11.

4. Daly, 13.

5. Michael Ford, *Father Mychal Judge: An Authentic American Hero* (Mahwah, NJ: Paulist Press, 2002), 49.

6. Daly, 19.

7. Daly, 301.

8. Ford, *Father Mychal Judge*, 54.

9. Ford, 55.

10. Ford, 54.

Chapter 2—pages 17–32

1. John Barone, interview with the author, September 9, 2019.

2. Eugene Dermody, Jr., interview with the author, September 4, 2019.

3. Dermody, interview.

4. Dermody, interview.

5. Joseph Tereskiewicz, interview with the author, September 13, 2019.

6. Tereskiewicz, interview.

7. Barone, interview.

8. Wilma Supik, "The Listening Priest," *The Record*, September 8, 1974, 25.

9. Michael Daly, *The Book of Mychal: The Surprising Life and Heroic Death of Father Mychal Judge* (New York: St. Martin's Press, 2008), 35.

10. Supik, "Listening Priest."

11. Michael Duffy, OFM, "Homily Preached at Funeral Mass for Fr. Mychal Judge, OFM," Franciscan Friars of the Holy Name Province, https://hnp.org/wp-content/uploads/2014/03/09-15-01-mjhomily.pdf.

12. Wilma Supik, "The Giving Priest," *The Record*, November 26, 1976, 45.

13. Michael Ford, *Father Mychal Judge: An Authentic American Hero* (Mahwah, NJ: Paulist Press, 2002), 22.

14. Brian Carroll, interview with the author, December 6, 2019.

15. Wilma Supik, "A Time for Hope," *The Record*, September 1, 1978, 47.

16. Daly, *Book of Mychal*, 41.

17. Supik, "Listening Priest."

18. Howard Prosnitz, "Beloved Priest Perishes in WTC Blasts," *The South Bergenite*, September 19, 2001, A1.

19. Jane McGuire, "Parish Thrives without Pastor," *The Record*, June 6, 1972, 64.

20. Duffy, "Homily Preached at Funeral Mass."

21. Daly, 62.

22. Supik, "Listening Priest."

23. Daly, 43–44.

24. Daly, 46.

25. Daly, 47.

26. Supik, "Listening Priest."

27. Daly, 67. When people who later identify as lesbian or gay are in the initial stages of coming to acceptance of their sexuality, it is not uncommon for them initially to acknowledge feelings for people of the same gender but to downplay their importance. While the existence of people who are truly bisexual is an acknowledged fact, it is also not uncommon for people who later identify as lesbian or gay to first identify as bisexual while they determine the truth of their identities.

28. Daly, 47.

29. Daly, 50.

30. Supik, "Giving Priest."

31. Daly, 59.

32. Reverend Hugh Hines, OFM, interview with the author, September 25, 2019.

33. Hines, interview.

34. Daly, 62.

Chapter 3—pages 33–46

1. Michael Daly, *The Book of Mychal: The Surprising Life and Heroic Death of Father Mychal Judge* (New York: St. Martin's Press, 2008), 250.

2. Brian Carroll, interview with the author, December 6, 2019.

3. Bob, interview with the author, December 3, 2019.

4. In 1976, John McNeill had written *The Church and the Homosexual*, the first comprehensive theological critique of Catholicism's disapproval of gay and lesbian sexual relationships. After several run-ins with the hierarchy, McNeill was dismissed from the Jesuits but continued his psychotherapy practice, primarily with gay men from religious backgrounds.

5. Daly, *Book of Mychal*, 91.

6. Michael Ford, *Father Mychal Judge: An Authentic American Hero* (Mahwah, NJ: Paulist Press, 2002), 75.

7. Reverend Fran Di Spigno, OFM, interview with the author, December 5, 2019.

8. Jennifer Senior, "The Firemen's Friar," *New York*, November 12, 2001, https://nymag.com/nymetro/news/sept11/features/5372/.

9. Senior, "Firemen's Friar."

10. Salvatore Sapienza, *Mychal's Prayer: Praying with Father Mychal Judge* (Saugatuck, MI: Tregatti Press, 2011), 7.

11. "We admitted we were powerless over alcohol—that our lives had become unmanageable."

12. Richard Rohr, OFM, *Eager to Love: The Alternative Way of Francis of Assisi* (Cincinnati: Franciscan Media, 2016), 19.

13. Rohr, 19–20.

14. Carroll, interview.

15. *Alcoholics Anonymous*, 4th ed. (New York: Alcoholics Anonymous World Services, 2001), 133.

16. Ford, *Father Mychal Judge*, 106.

17. Ford, 97.

18. Ford, 102.

19. Ford, 101.

20. Daly, *Book of Mychal*, 72.

21. Daly, 73.

22. Rohr, *Eager to Love*, 30.

23. Rohr, 32.

24. Rohr, 28.

25. Rohr, 26–27.

Chapter 4—pages 47–64

1. Michael Daly, *The Book of Mychal: The Surprising Life and Heroic Death of Father Mychal Judge* (New York: St. Martin's Press, 2008), 81.

2. Reverend Hugh Hines, OFM, interview with the author, September 25, 2019.

3. Michael Ford, *Father Mychal Judge: An Authentic American Hero* (Mahwah, NJ: Paulist Press, 2002), 130.

4. Hines, interview.

5. Salvatore Sapienza, *Mychal's Prayer: Praying with Father Mychal Judge* (Saugatuck, MI: Tregatti Press, 2011), 43–44.

6. Daly, *Book of Mychal*, 121.

7. The most common usage during Judge's lifetime to describe what is today referred to as the lesbian, gay, bisexual, transgender, and queer (LGBTQ) community was LGB or LGBT. In this book, I will employ the acronym appropriate to the particular historical context.

8. Congregation for the Doctrine of the Faith, Declaration on Certain Questions Concerning Sexual Ethics *Persona Humana*, December 29, 1975, VIII.

9. Washington State Catholic Conference, *Prejudice Against Homosexuals and the Ministry of the Church* (1983).

10. Salvatore Sapienza, interview with the author, September 12, 2019.

11. *Democracy Now!*, "Saint of 9/11: Remembering NY Fire Chaplain Mychal Judge, Gay Catholic Priest Killed at WTC," transcript, September 6, 2011, https://www.democracynow.org/2011/9/6/saint_of_9_11_remembering_ny.

12. See Larry McShane, "Chaplain's Status Has Life After Death," *Los Angeles Times*, January 6, 2002, https://www.latimes.com/archives/la-xpm-2002-jan-06-mn-20642-story.html: "'Father Judge was neither out nor closeted,' one friend told The Advocate, the national gay magazine. 'He knew how to walk that fine line.'"

13. Ford, *Father Mychal Judge*, 120.

14. Congregation for the Doctrine of the Faith, "Letter to the Bishops of the Catholic Church on the Pastoral Care of Homosexual Persons," October 1, 1986, 3, https://www.vatican.va/roman_curia/congregations/cfaith/documents/rc_con_cfaith_doc_19861001_homosexual-persons_en.html.

15. Congregation for the Doctrine of the Faith, "Letter to the Bishops," 10: "It is deplorable that homosexual persons have been and are the object of violent malice in speech or in action. Such treatment deserves condemnation from the church's pastors wherever it occurs. It reveals a kind of disregard for others that endangers the most fundamental principles of a healthy society. The intrinsic dignity of each person must always be respected in word, in action, and in law.

"But the proper reaction to crimes committed against homosexual persons should not be to claim that the homosexual condition is not disordered. When such a claim is made and when homosexual activity is consequently condoned, or when civil legislation is introduced to protect behavior to which no one has any conceivable right, neither the Church nor society at large should be surprised when other distorted notions and practices gain ground, and irrational and violent reactions increase."

16. Bernárd J. Lynch, *If It Wasn't Love: Sex, Death and God* (Winchester, UK: Circle Books, 2012).

17. Congregation for the Doctrine of the Faith, "Letter to the Bishops," 17: "All support should be withdrawn from any organizations which seek to undermine the teaching of the Church, which are ambiguous about it, or which neglect it entirely. Such support, or even the semblance of such support, can be gravely misinterpreted.

Special attention should be given to the practice of scheduling religious services and to the use of Church buildings by these groups, including the facilities of Catholic schools and colleges. To some, such permission to use Church property may seem only just and charitable; but in reality it is contradictory to the purpose for which these institutions were founded, it is misleading and often scandalous."

18. Ford, *Father Mychal Judge*, 123–24.

19. Daly, *Book of Mychal*, 85.

20. St. Vincent's Catholic Medical Center in Greenwich Village, the heart of the city's gay community at the time, was the first Catholic hospital to admit an AIDS patient. It was only the second hospital in the country to do so. St. Vincent's would become known as "Ground Zero for HIV/AIDS" and Judge would spend a great deal of his time there, too, ministering to patients. For some history about Catholic involvement with HIV/AIDS ministry, see Michael J. O'Loughlin, "The Secret History of Catholic Caregivers and the AIDS Epidemic," *America*, May 31, 2019, https://www.americamagazine.org/faith/2019/05/31/secret-history-catholic-caregivers-and-aids-epidemic, and O'Loughlin, "The Catholic Nun Who Came to New York to Confront the AIDS Crisis," *Daily Beast*, January 21, 2019, https://www.thedailybeast.com/the-catholic-nun-who-came-to-new-york-to-confront-the-aids-crisis.

21. Daly, *Book of Mychal*, 85.

22. Daly, 86.

23. Daly, 91.

24. Daly, 90.

25. Sapienza, interview.

26. Sapienza, interview.

27. Sapienza, interview.

28. Sapienza, interview.

29. *Saint of 9/11*, directed by Glenn Holsten (Santa Fe, NM: Equality Forum, 2006).

30. Daly, *Book of Mychal*, 142.

31. *Saint of 9/11* film.

32. Daly, *Book of Mychal*, 94.

33. Taming the Wolf Institute (blog), "Seeing the Divine in the Other: Saint Francis and the Leper," n.d., https://tamingthewolf.com/seeing-the-divine-in-the-other-saint-francis-and-the-leper/.

Chapter 5—pages 65–78

1. Michael Daly, *The Book of Mychal: The Surprising Life and Heroic Death of Father Mychal Judge* (New York: St. Martin's Press, 2008), 111.

2. Daly, 110.

3. Daly, 112.

4. Daly, 105.

5. Lieutenant David Fullam, interview with the author, September 25, 2019.

6. Jennifer Senior, "The Firemen's Friar," *New York*, November 12, 2001, https://nymag.com/nymetro/news/sept11/features/5372/.

7. Daly, *Book of Mychal*, 165–66.

8. Daly, 168.

9. Barbara Bradley Hagerty, "Memories of Sept. 11's First Recorded Casualty Endure," *All Things Considered*, September 5, 2011, https://www.npr.org/2011/09/05/140154885/memories-of-sept-11s-first-casualty-burn-bright.

10. Michael Ford, *Father Mychal Judge: An Authentic American Hero* (Mahwah, NJ: Paulist Press, 2002), 147.

11. Daly, *Book of Mychal*, 208–9.

12. Daly, 267.

13. Daly, 169.

14. Daly, 159.

15. Daly, 138.

16. Daly, 279.

17. Fullam, interview.

18. Carol Walsh, interview with the author, December 3, 2019.

19. Daly, *Book of Mychal*, 118.

20. Daly, 254.

Chapter 6—pages 79–99

1. Michael Ford, *Father Mychal Judge: An Authentic American Hero* (Mahwah, NJ: Paulist Press, 2002), 4–5.

2. Ford, 5.

3. Wilma Supik, "A Time for Hope," *The Record*, September 1, 1978, 47.

4. Johann Christoph Arnold, "Steven McDonald's Story," Plough Publishing, February 26, 2013, https://www.plough.com/en/articles /steven-mcdonalds-story, from Arnold, *Why Forgive?* (Walden, NY: Plough, 2010).

5. Arnold, "Steven McDonald's Story."

6. *Democracy Now!*, "Saint of 9/11: Remembering NY Fire Chaplain Mychal Judge, Gay Catholic Priest Killed at WTC," transcript, September 6, 2011, https://www.democracynow.org/2011/9/6 /saint_of_9_11_remembering_ny.

7. Michael Daly, "The Cop Who Forgave His Killer," *The Daily Beast*, January 15, 2017, https://www.thedailybeast.com/the-cop -who-forgave-his-killer.

8. Ford, *Father Mychal Judge*, 163.

9. Daly, "Cop Who Forgave His Killer."

10. James Barron, "Beer Shower and Boos for Dinkins at Irish Parade," *New York Times*, March 17, 1991, 1, https://www.nytimes .com/1991/03/17/nyregion/beer-shower-and-boos-for-dinkins-at-irish -parade.html.

11. Michael Daly, *The Book of Mychal: The Surprising Life and Heroic Death of Father Mychal Judge* (New York: St. Martin's Press, 2008), 133–34.

12. Francis X. Clines, "Irish March Up the Avenue, Gay Protesters at Bay," *New York Times*, March 18, 1993, A1, https://www.nytimes .com/1993/03/18/nyregion/irish-march-up-the-avenue-gay-protesters -at-bay.html.

13. Ford, *Father Mychal Judge*, 183.

14. Salvatore Sapienza, interview with the author, September 12, 2019.

15. Clines, "Irish March Up the Avenue."

16. Daly, *Book of Mychal*, 120.

17. Daly, 281.

18. Daly, 314.

19. Daly, 314.

20. Daly, 308–9.

21. Daly, 257.

22. Daly, 257.

23. Daly, 257.

24. Daly, 258.

25. Daly, 259.

26. Daly, 260.

27. Daly, 300.

28. Daly, 55.

29. Daly, 252–53.

30. Jennifer Senior, "The Firemen's Friar," *New York*, November 12, 2001, https://nymag.com/nymetro/news/sept11/features/5372/.

Chapter 7—pages 100–113

1. Michael Daly, *The Book of Mychal: The Surprising Life and Heroic Death of Father Mychal Judge* (New York: St. Martin's Press, 2008), 320.

2. Michael Ford, *Father Mychal Judge: An Authentic American Hero* (Mahwah, NJ: Paulist Press, 2002), 189–90.

3. Ford, 190–91.

4. Ford, 193.

5. Brian Carroll, interview with the author, December 6, 2019.

6. Reverend Fran Di Spigno, OFM, interview with the author, December 5, 2019.

7. Daly, *Book of Mychal*, 327.

8. Barbara Bradley Hagerty, "Memories of Sept. 11's First Recorded Casualty Endure," *All Things Considered*, September 5, 2011, https://www.npr.org/2011/09/05/140154885/memories-of-sept-11s-first-casualty-burn-bright.

9. Anna Mehler Paperny, "For Five Men, Tragedy Remains over Photo of 9/11's First Casualty," *The Globe and Mail*, September 1, 2011, https://www.theglobeandmail.com/news/world/for-five-men-tragedy-remains-over-photo-of-911s-first-casualty/article592945/.

11. Hagerty, "Memories of Sept. 11's."

12. Daly, *Book of Mychal*, 329.

13. Daly, 332.

14. Daly, 335.

15. Daly, 336.

16. NPR Staff, "Slain Priest: 'Bury His Heart, But Not His Love,' " *Morning Edition*, September 9, 2011, https://www.npr.org/2011/09/09/140293993/slain-priest-bury-his-heart-but-not-his-love.

17. Daly, *Book of Mychal*, 339–40.

18. Paperny, "For Five Men, Tragedy Remains."

19. Paperny.

20. Daly, *Book of Mychal,* 340.

21. Daly, 347.

22. *Saint of 9/11*, directed by Glenn Holsten (Santa Fe, NM: Equality Forum, 2006).

23. Daly, *Book of Mychal*, 355.

24. *Saint of 9/11* film.

25. Carroll, interview.

26. Michael Duffy, OFM, "Homily Preached at Funeral Mass for Fr. Mychal Judge, OFM," Franciscan Friars of the Holy Name Province, https://hnp.org/wp-content/uploads/2014/03/09-15-01-mjhomily.pdf.

Chapter 8—pages 114–33

1. "For Whom the Bell Tolls, Part II," *Village Voice*, September 18, 2001, https://www.villagevoice.com/2001/09/18/for-whom-the-bell-tolls-part-ii/.

2. Andy Humm, "A Love Supreme," *Village Voice*, October 9, 2001, https://www.villagevoice.com/2001/10/09/a-love-supreme/.

3. Daniel Burke, "Fallen 9/11 Priest Emerges as an Icon for Gay Catholics," *National Catholic Reporter*, September 9, 2011, https://www.ncronline.org/news/people/fallen-911-priest-emerges-icon-gay-catholics.

4. Michael Daly, *The Book of Mychal: The Surprising Life and Heroic Death of Father Mychal Judge* (New York: St. Martin's Press, 2008), 144.

5. Aidan Lonergan, "Campaign Underway to Make Irish-American Priest Who Died in 9/11 Attacks the World's First 'Gay Saint,' " *The Irish Post*, September 25, 2017, https://www.irishpost.com/news/campaign-underway-to-make-irish-american-priest-who-died-in-911-attacks-the-worlds-first-gay-saint-134933.

6. Daniel J. Wakin, "Killed on 9/11, Fire Chaplain Becomes Larger than Life," *New York Times*, September 27, 2002, https://www.nytimes.com/2002/09/27/nyregion/killed-on-9-11-fire-chaplain-becomes-larger-than-life.html.

7. Dennis Lynch, "A September 11th Hijacking," Catholic Online, https://www.catholic.org/featured/headline.php?ID=19.

8. Salvatore Sapienza, interview with the author, September 12, 2019.

9. Michael Ford, *Father Mychal Judge: An Authentic American Hero* (Mahwah, NJ: Paulist Press, 2002).

10. *Saint of 9/11*, directed by Glenn Holsten (Santa Fe, NM: Equality Forum, 2006).

11. Daly, *Book of Mychal*, 300.

12. Daly, 302.

13. Daly, 302–3, 305.

14. Daly, 117.

15. Brian Carroll, interview with the author, December 6, 2019.

16. Daly, *Book of Mychal*, 121, 127.

17. Daly, 117.

18. Sean Kirst, "Mychal Judge: Celebrating the Whole Person at All Saints," Syracuse.com, October 31, 2011, https://www.syracuse.com/kirst/2011/10/post_211.html.

19. Congregation for Catholic Education, "Instruction Concerning the Criteria for the Discernment of Vocations with Regard to Persons with Homosexual Tendencies in View of Their Admission to the Seminary and to Holy Orders," August 31, 2005, http://www.vatican.va/roman_curia/congregations/ccatheduc/documents/rc_con_ccatheduc_doc_20051104_istruzione_en.html.

20. Congregation for the Clergy, "The Gift of the Priestly Vocation," December 8, 2016, 199, http://www.clerus.va/content/dam/clerus/Ratio%20Fundamentalis/The%20Gift%20of%20the%20Priestly%20Vocation.pdf.

21. "Estratto da 'La forza della vocazione': Papa Francesco: no ai sacerdoti omosessuali" ["Excerpt from 'The Power of Vocation': Pope Francis: No to Homosexual Priests"], *Avvenire*, December 1, 2018, https://www.avvenire.it/papa/pagine/libro-la-forza-della-vocazione-estratto.

22. Daly, *Book of Mychal*, 304–5.

23. New York Press Club, "NYPC Journalism Awards," https://www.nypressclub.org/new-entry-2/.

24. Sean Kirst, "Remembering Mychal Judge: A Monumental Quest at a Parish Sculpted by Compassion," Syracuse.com, July 26, 2011, https://www.syracuse.com/kirst/2011/07/post_181.html.

25. Pope Francis, Apostolic letter *Maiorem hac dilectionem*, July 11, 2017, https://www.vatican.va/content/francesco/en/motu_proprio/documents/papa-francesco-motu-proprio_20170711_maiorem-hac-dilectionem.html.

26. See https://www.newwaysministry.org/judge.

27. Wakin, "Killed on 9/11."

28. David Crary, "Admirers Still Urging Sainthood for Chaplain Killed on 9/11," *Associated Press*, September 4, 2021.

Postscript—pages 134–37

1. Michael Daly, *The Book of Mychal: The Surprising Life and Heroic Death of Father Mychal Judge* (New York: St. Martin's Press, 2008), 300.

Bibliography

Alcoholics Anonymous. 4th ed. New York: Alcoholics Anonymous World Services, 2001.

Arnold, Johann Christoph. "Steven McDonald's Story." Plough Publishing. February 26, 2013. https://www.plough.com /en/articles/steven-mcdonalds-story. (From Arnold, *Why Forgive?* [Walden, NY: Plough, 2010].)

Avvenire. "Estratto da 'La forza della vocazione': Papa Francesco: no ai sacerdoti omosessuali" ["Excerpt from 'The Power of Vocation': Pope Francis: No to Homosexual Priests"]. December 1, 2018. https://www.avvenire.it/papa/pagine /libro-la-forza-della-vocazione-estratto.

Barron, James. "Beer Shower and Boos for Dinkins at Irish Parade." *New York Times.* March 17, 1991. https://www .nytimes.com/1991/03/17/nyregion/beer-shower-and-boos -for-dinkins-at-irish-parade.html.

Blomquist, David. "Anguish, Serenity: Reflections of a Friar." *The (Hackensack) Record.* April 4, 1985: 13.

Burke, Daniel. "Fallen 9/11 Priest Emerges as an Icon for Gay Catholics." *National Catholic Reporter.* September 9, 2011. https://www.ncronline.org/news/people/fallen-911 -priest-emerges-icon-gay-catholics.

Clines, Francis X. "Irish March Up the Avenue, Gay Protesters at Bay." *New York Times.* March 18, 1993. https://www .nytimes.com/1993/03/18/nyregion/irish-march-up-the -avenue-gay-protesters-at-bay.html.

Congregation for Catholic Education. "Instruction Concerning the Criteria for the Discernment of Vocations with Regard to Persons with Homosexual Tendencies in View of Their Admission to the Seminary and to Holy Orders." August 31, 2005. http://www.vatican.va/roman_curia/congregations /ccatheduc/documents/rc_con_ccatheduc_doc_20051104 _istruzione_en.html.

Congregation for the Clergy. "The Gift of the Priestly Vocation." December 8, 2016. http://www.clerus.va/content/dam /clerus/Ratio%20Fundamentalis/The%20Gift%20of%20 the%20Priestly%20Vocation.pdf.

Congregation for the Doctrine of the Faith. Declaration on Certain Questions Concerning Sexual Ethics *Persona Humana*. December 29, 1975.

Congregation for the Doctrine of the Faith. "Letter to the Bishops of the Catholic Church on the Pastoral Care of Homosexual Persons." October 1, 1986. https://www.vatican .va/roman_curia/congregations/cfaith/documents/rc_con _cfaith_doc_19861001_homosexual-persons_en.html.

Crary, David. "Admirers Still Urging Sainthood for Chaplain Killed on 9/11." *Associated Press*. September 4, 2021.

Daly, Michael. *The Book of Mychal: The Surprising Life and Heroic Death of Father Mychal Judge*. New York: St. Martin's Press, 2008.

Daly, Michael. "The Cop Who Forgave His Killer." *The Daily Beast*. January 15, 2017. https://www.thedailybeast.com /the-cop-who-forgave-his-killer.

Democracy Now! "Saint of 9/11: Remembering NY Fire Chaplain Mychal Judge, Gay Catholic Priest Killed at WTC," transcript. September 6, 2011. https://www.democracynow .org/2011/9/6/saint_of_9_11_remembering_ny.

Duffy, OFM, Michael. "Homily Preached at Funeral Mass for Fr. Mychal Judge, OFM." Franciscan Friars of the Holy Name Province. https://hnp.org/wp-content/uploads/2014 /03/09-15-01-mjhomily.pdf.

Ford, Michael. *Father Mychal Judge: An Authentic American Hero*. Mahwah, NJ: Paulist Press, 2002.

Hagerty, Barbara Bradley. "Memories of Sept. 11's First Recorded Casualty Endure." *All Things Considered.* September 5, 2011. https://www.npr.org/2011/09/05/140154885 /memories-of-sept-11s-first-casualty-burn-bright.

Humm, Andy. "A Love Supreme." *Village Voice.* October 9, 2001. https://www.villagevoice.com/2001/10/09/a-love-supreme/.

Kirst, Sean. "Mychal Judge: Celebrating the Whole Person at All Saints." Syracuse.com. October 31, 2011. https://www .syracuse.com/kirst/2011/10/post_211.html.

Kirst, Sean. "Remembering Mychal Judge: A Monumental Quest at a Parish Sculpted by Compassion." Syracuse.com. July 26, 2011. https://www.syracuse.com/kirst/2011/07/post _181.html.

Lonergan, Aidan. "Campaign Underway to Make Irish-American Priest Who Died in 9/11 Attacks the World's First 'Gay Saint.'" *The Irish Post.* September 25, 2017. https://www .irishpost.com/news/campaign-underway-to-make-irish -american-priest-who-died-in-911-attacks-the-worlds-first -gay-saint-134933.

Lynch, Bernárd J. *If It Wasn't Love: Sex, Death and God.* Winchester, UK: Circle Books, 2012.

Lynch, Dennis. "A September 11th Hijacking." Catholic Online. https://www.catholic.org/featured/headline.php?ID=19.

McGuire, Jane. "Parish Thrives without Pastor." *The Record.* June 6, 1972.

McShane, Larry. "Chaplain's Status Has Life After Death." *Los Angeles Times.* January 6, 2002. https://www.latimes.com /archives/la-xpm-2002-jan-06-mn-20642-story.html.

New Ways Ministry. "It's Time to Canonize Fr. Mychal Judge." https://www.newwaysministry.org/advocate/judge/.

New York Press Club. "NYPC Journalism Awards." https://www .nypressclub.org/new-entry-2/.

NPR Staff. "Slain Priest: 'Bury His Heart, But Not His Love.'" *Morning Edition.* September 9, 2011. https://www.npr .org/2011/09/09/140293993/slain-priest-bury-his-heart -but-not-his-love.

O'Loughlin, Michael J. "The Catholic Nun Who Came to New York to Confront the AIDS Crisis." *Daily Beast*. January 21, 2019. https://www.thedailybeast.com/the-catholic-nun-who-came-to-new-york-to-confront-the-aids-crisis.

O'Loughlin, Michael J. "The Secret History of Catholic Caregivers and the AIDS Epidemic." *America*. May 31, 2019. https://www.americamagazine.org/faith/2019/05/31/secret-history-catholic-caregivers-and-aids-epidemic.

Paperny, Anna Mehler. "For Five Men, Tragedy Remains over Photo of 9/11's First Casualty." *The Globe and Mail*. September 1, 2011. https://www.theglobeandmail.com/news/world/for-five-men-tragedy-remains-over-photo-of-911s-first-casualty/article592945/.

The Paterson News. "Police Besiege Carlstadt Man." May 20, 1974: 2.

Pope Francis. Apostolic letter *Maiorem hac dilectionem*. July 11, 2017. https://www.vatican.va/content/francesco/en/motu_proprio/documents/papa-francesco-motu-proprio_20170711_maiorem-hac-dilectionem.html.

Prosnitz, Howard. "Beloved Priest Perishes in WTC Blasts." *The South Bergenite*. September 19, 2001.

Rohr, OFM, Fr. Richard. *Eager to Love: The Alternative Way of Francis of Assisi*. Cincinnati: Franciscan Media, 2014.

Saint of 9/11. Directed by Glenn Holsten. Santa Fe, NM: Equality Forum, 2006.

Sapienza, Salvatore. *Mychal's Prayer: Praying with Father Mychal Judge*. Saugatuck, MI: Tregatti Press, 2011.

Senior, Jennifer. "The Firemen's Friar." *New York*. November 12, 2001. https://nymag.com/nymetro/news/sept11/features/5372/.

Supik, Wilma. "The Giving Priest." *The Record*. November 26, 1976.

Supik, Wilma. "The Listening Priest." *The Record*. September 8, 1974.

Supik, Wilma. "A Time for Hope." *The Record*. September 1, 1978.

Taming the Wolf Institute (blog). "Seeing the Divine in the Other: Saint Francis and the Leper." https://tamingthewolf.com /seeing-the-divine-in-the-other-saint-francis-and-the-leper/.

Village Voice. "For Whom the Bell Tolls, Part II." September 18, 2001. https://www.villagevoice.com/2001/09/18/for -whom-the-bell-tolls-part-ii/.

Wakin, Daniel J. "Killed on 9/11, Fire Chaplain Becomes Larger than Life." *New York Times*. September 27, 2002. https:// www.nytimes.com/2002/09/27/nyregion/killed-on-9-11 -fire-chaplain-becomes-larger-than-life.html.

Washington State Catholic Conference. *Prejudice Against Homosexuals and the Ministry of the Church*. 1983.

Index